W9-AQT-707

THE ROLE OF AMERICAN INTELLIGENCE ORGANIZATIONS

edited by GEORGE WITTMAN

THE REFERENCE SHELF
Volume 48   Number 5

THE H. W. WILSON COMPANY
New York   1976

THE REFERENCE SHELF

The books in this series contain reprints of articles, excerpts from books, and addresses on current issues and social trends in the United States and other countries. There are six separately bound numbers in each volume, all of which are generally published in the same calendar year. One number is a collection of recent speeches; each of the others is devoted to a single subject and gives background information and discussion from various points of view, concluding with a comprehensive bibliography. Books in the series may be purchased individually or on subscription.

Library of Congress Cataloging in Publication Data
Main entry under title:

The Role of American intelligence organizations.

(The Reference shelf ; v. 48, no. 5)
Bibliography: p.
1. Intelligence service—United States. I. Wittman, George. II. Series.
JK468.I6R64   353.008′92   76-54775
ISBN 0-8242-0599-5

PREFACE

In April 1976 the Senate Select Committee to Study Governmental Operations With Respect to Intelligence Activities (often referred to as the Select Committee on Intelligence or as the Church Committee because it is chaired by Senator Frank Church, Democrat of Idaho) issued its final report. It concluded:

"Over the past thirty years the United States has developed an institution and a corps of individuals who constitute the U.S. intelligence-profession. The question remains as to how the institution and the individual will be best utilized."

This question had already been posed repeatedly in one form or another as, in the wake of Watergate, more and more people with knowledge of the inner workings of the American intelligence establishment "went public" with what they knew. Newspaper articles, books, and congressional investigations not only revealed a whole catalog of illegal or unauthorized activities, but also made clear certain characteristics of the intelligence community: structural confusion caused by the fact that the CIA not only coordinates the gathering of foreign intelligence but actually produces most of it itself; a "club membership" atmosphere in which only special members of Congress were allowed to know about intelligence operations of which even the Executive branch, which authorized the activities, remained in the dark; and an attitude among intelligence professionals that personal success was more likely to be achieved through organizational loyalty than through any larger concern for "national interest." None of these char-

3

acteristics is unusual in a government service or, for that matter, in any large human organization.

But the nation had expected better-than-average behavior from the intelligence elite, the sole element in our government authorized by law to perform covert intelligence tasks. Watergate and the ensuing investigations showed that the intelligence professionals who had the responsibility to manage these secret matters—both at home and abroad—had failed to live up to public expectations. And it was not only the professionals who had failed—officials, both elected and appointed, in the White House and in Congress, had here failed to act as the public expected.

In its final recommendations, Senator Church's Select Committee on Intelligence Activities recognized these basic failures of responsibility. Broad-ranging suggestions were made affecting the organization and character of the entire field of foreign-intelligence gathering, analysis, and operations. At the same time the committee moved to establish a new permanent committee on intelligence which would assume the previously neglected duty of oversight over the nation's intelligence apparatus. The full Senate approved the creation of this new committee and additionally accepted the expanded character of the new body that, for the first time, gave the Congress a role in the formulation of both strategic and tactical policy in this area.

In this compilation, an attempt has been made to provide the reader not only with a selection of illuminating contemporary opinion, but also with the academic, historical, and operational background that is necessary for a consideration of the proper role of intelligence agencies in American society. The first section presents background information, including an analysis of what intelligence is, the history of its development in the United States, discussion of the need for such activity, and a statement of the statutory function of CIA. The second supplies commentary on recent revelations concerning the intelligence community and investigations of that service. The third deals with the aftermath of the revelations: proposed reforms and the establishing of true oversight.

However, there are significant areas on which little or nothing has been published, and the lack of such commentary points up the incomplete nature of the public exploration of foreign intelligence—perhaps even an unwillingness or an inability to probe further.

First, there is the question whether or not the United States actually should be in the covert foreign-intelligence business. Most observers immediately answer in the affirmative, holding that such activity is the natural requirement of any nation; others, no more or less "moral," believe strongly that such efforts are completely inconsistent with the intent and character of our democratic nation. The latter are distinctly in the minority. Yet the arguments for and against covert foreign-intelligence capability have not been well drawn. Published comment against all covert intelligence has been limited to polemics rather than careful analysis. This area begs substantive investigation and documentation.

Another important question deals with the different role of covert intelligence in time of war: Is the difference a matter of degree? What is allowable in a war situation that is not allowable in time of peace?

Finally, and perhaps most significantly, what is the role and what are the responsibilities of the individual professional? With all the debate on the need for congressional oversight and appropriate checks and balances to guide and control an American foreign-intelligence system, there has been virtually nothing said of the ultimate control—the people who perform on all levels. What is demanded of them? What should be demanded of them? Are they to be merely soldiers following orders? Can there be an intelligence ethic?

The reader should be aware that these critical questions, not sufficiently addressed by the press or the public, need to be explored to complete the frame of analysis on which this compendium is based.

The editor wishes to thank the authors and publishers of the selections which follow for permission to reprint them in this compilation.

GEORGE WITTMAN

November 1976

NOTE TO THE READER

For further information on FBI and CIA activities, particularly in the domestic intelligence area, see Section III, "The Role of the FBI and the CIA," in *The Right to Privacy*, edited by Grant S. McClellan (Reference Shelf, Volume 48, Number 1) published in March 1976.

CONTENTS

III.   AFTER THE INVESTIGATION: OVERSIGHT AND RE-
       FORM

I. INTELLIGENCE: WHAT IT IS AND HOW IT EVOLVED IN THE UNITED STATES

EDITOR'S INTRODUCTION

The four selections that constitute this first section provide a background for the study of American intelligence. The emphasis in the selection is on the covert aspects of this activity. The first piece, "Intelligence Is Knowledge," is a chapter from Sherman Kent's *Strategic Intelligence for American World Policy*, published nearly twenty-five years before the Watergate disclosures of 1973. Professor Kent's three-part characterization of intelligence as knowledge, organization, and activity is often considered the classical definition. The second excerpt is taken from *The Craft of Intelligence*, by Allen Dulles, director of the CIA from 1953 to 1961. This review of the antecedents of modern American intelligence lends insight into the man who, above all others, characterized the leadership of American intelligence agencies since World War II.

The third selection is a presentation by John A. McCone, former CIA director, explaining CIA activities. Lastly, there is a selection from Professor Harry Howe Ransom's *The Intelligence Establishment* outlining the CIA's statutory functions as set out in the National Security Act of 1947.

INTELLIGENCE IS KNOWLEDGE [1]

Intelligence means knowledge. If it cannot be stretched to mean all knowledge, at least it means an amazing bulk and assortment of knowledge. This book deals with only a fraction of the total, but probably the most important fraction. It deals with the part, known to the intelligence trade as "high-level foreign positive intelligence." This phrase is short for the kind of knowledge our state must possess regarding other states in order to assure itself that its cause will not suffer nor its undertakings fail because its statesmen and soldiers plan and act in ignorance. This is the knowledge upon which we base our high-level national policy toward the other states of the world.

Notice what is being excluded. First, all knowledge of our own domestic scene is being left out. Foreign positive intelligence is truly "foreign" in purpose, scope, and substance. It is not concerned with what goes on in the United States or in its territories and possessions. Second, all knowledge of the sort which lies behind the police function is excluded. The word *positive* comes into the phrase to denote that the intelligence in question is not so-called "counterintelligence" and counterespionage nor any other sort of intelligence designed to uncover domestically-produced traitors or imported foreign agents. The words *high-level* are there to exclude what is called "operational" intelligence, tactical intelligence, and the intelligence of small military formations in battle known as combat intelligence. What is left is the knowledge indispensable to our welfare

[1] Selections from Chapter I of *Strategic Intelligence for American World Policy*, by Sherman Kent, historian. Princeton University Press. '49. p. 3-10. Copyright © 1949 by Princeton University Press; Princeton Paperback 1966. Reprinted by permission of Princeton University Press. The author was a professor of history at Yale before entering government service. Formerly on the staff of the National War College, he was at one time director of the Office of Research and Intelligence, U.S. Department of State.

and security. It is both the constructive knowledge with which we can work toward peace and freedom throughout the world, and the knowledge necessary to the defense of our country and its ideals. Some of this knowledge may be acquired through clandestine means, but the bulk of it must be had through unromantic open-and-above-board observation and research.

It should be borne in mind . . . that the intelligence activity consists basically of two sorts of operation. I have called them the *surveillance operation,* by which I mean the many ways by which the contemporary world is put under close and systematic observation, and the *research operation.* By the latter I mean the attempts to establish meaningful patterns out of what was observed in the past and attempts to get meaning out of what appears to be going on now. The two operations are virtually inseparable, though for administrative and other reasons they are often physically separated. In actual practice there are generally two different staffs each of which cultivates the respective specialisms of surveillance and research. But however far apart they get on the administrative diagram or in the development of their own techniques they are closely bound together by their common devotion to the production of knowledge.

How describe this kind of knowledge? There are at least two ways. One way is to treat high-level foreign positive intelligence as the substance of humanity and nature—abroad. This involves an almost endless listing of the components of humanity and nature. The listings can be alphabetical or topical. Whichever, it runs to hundreds of pages and would ill serve the interests of the readers of this sort of book.

The other way, and the one I have adopted, is neither alphabetical nor topical. It might be called functional. It starts from the premise that our state, in order to survive in a world of competing states, must have two sorts of state policy. The one is its own self-initiated, positive, outgoing policy, undertaken in the interests of a better world order and a higher degree of national prosperity. The other is its defensive-protective policy necessarily undertaken to counter those policies of other states which are inimical to our national aspirations. This second kind of policy might better be called our policy for national security. I make this artificial distinction, between positive and security policies, for purposes of the present analysis.

Consider our positive policy first. To be effective, its framers, planners, and implementers must be able to select the proper instrumentality of suasion from a long list of possibles. Will it be a resolution in the UN, will it be diplomacy, will it be political and economic inducement or threat, will it be propaganda or information, will it be force, will it be a combination of several? The framers, planners, and implementers must also know where, how, and when to apply the instrumentality of their choice. Now neither the selecting nor the applying can be done without reference to the party of the second part. Before the policy leaders do either they would be well advised to know:

> *how* the other country is going to receive the policy in question and what it is prepared to use to counter it;
> *what* the other country lacks in the way of countering force (i.e.) its specific vulnerabilities;
> *what* it is doing to array its protective force; and
> *what* it is doing, or indeed can do, to mend its specific vulnerabilities.

Thus our policy leaders find themselves in need of a great deal of knowledge about foreign countries. They need knowledge which is complete, which is accurate, which is delivered on time, and which is capable of serving as a basis for action. To put their positive policy into effect they should first and foremost know about other countries as objective entities. For example, they must know about:

1. the physiques of these countries, that is, their natural topography and environment and the multiform permanent structures which man has added to the landscape (his cities, his agricultural and industrial enterprises, his transportation facilities, and so on)
2. their people—how many; how they are settled; how occupied
3. the status of the arts, sciences, and technologies of these people (and I would include in this the status of their armed forces)
4. the character of their political systems, their economies, their social groupings, their codes of morality, and the dynamic interrelations which prevail among all these

Armed with this knowledge the leaders of positive policy may go forward assured at least that, if they fail, their failure will not be chargeable to their ignorance.

Secondly, consider our other sort of policy, that is, our policy concerned with the maintenance of the national security. In the interests of security our policy leaders must make constant provision for the positive policies of *other* states. Some of these policies we will have to regard as hostile to our interests and we must take steps to block them. Some, we may wish to meet half way. To frame and operate this kind of security policy we must have a second large class of information about foreign countries, and again the knowledge must be complete, accurate, timely, and capable of serving as a basis for action. We must know the nature and weight of the instrumentalities which these other countries can summon in behalf of their own policies, and we must know the direction those policies are likely to take. We must know this not only so that we will not be taken by surprise, but also so that we will be in a position of defensive or offensive readiness when the policy is launched. When you know such things you know a good deal about the other country's *strategic stature*. . . . And on the theory that there is a relationship between what a country adopts as an objective and what it thinks it can expect to accomplish, knowledge of strategic stature constitutes, in some degree at least, knowledge of the other country's probable intentions.

From the foregoing it can be seen that my first class of information to be acquired is essentially descriptive and reportorial. It is descriptive of the relatively changeless things like terrain, hydrography, and climate. It is descriptive of the changeable but no less permanent things like population. It is descriptive, too, of the more transient man-made phenomena such as governmental or economic structures. With this kind of knowledge our leaders can draft the guide lines of our positive policy, of our peace-time and wartime strategy.

The second class of information to be acquired deals with the future and its possibilities and probabilities: how another country may shape its internal forces to service its foreign policy or strategy; how it may try to use these strengths against us, when, where, and with what effectiveness. Where the first was descriptive, this is speculative and evaluative.

With these classes of things to be known, then, we may perceive the statics, the dynamics, and the potentials of other countries; we will perceive the established things, the presently going-on things, and probable things of the future. Taken together these make up the subject matter of what I have called high-level foreign positive intelligence, or as I shall call it henceforth—strategic intelligence. Incidentally, they also indicate the three main forms in which strategic intelligence is turned out by intelligence organizations. These forms are: the *basic descriptive form,* the *current reportorial form,* and the *speculative-evaluative form.*

Here is the first place where I will depart from some of the accepted usages of the intelligence language. I take this departure . . . because of the large confusion one encounters in the lexicon of the trade. In the trade, what I have called the basic descriptive form is variously called basic research, fundamental research, basic data, monographic data, etc. What I call the current reportorial form goes by such names as current intelligence, current evaluations, current appreciations, reports, cable material, hot intelligence, etc. What I call the speculative-evaluative form is known as estimates, strategic estimates, evaluations, staff intelligence, capabilities intelligence, and so on.

On the theory that the consumers of intelligence are interested in things of the past, present, and future, I have adopted the element of time as the element of overruling importance. This permits an easy and consistent arrangement of the subject matter of intelligence and permits one to postpone cataloguing this subject matter according to use-to-be-served, consumer, etc. until a later and more appropriate stage. Few intelligence devotees have done this in the past. Far too many of them in making up their categories of the kinds of intelligence have deferred to several factors of discrimination in the same list. Thus you may find important directives of the intelligence brotherhood which contain a list of the kinds of intelligence looking something like this: (1) Basic research, (2) Strategic intelligence, (3) Technical intelligence, (4) Counterintelligence, (5) Tactical intelligence, (6) Capabilities and estimates intelligence. Such categories are by no means mutually exclusive nor are they consistent with one another. . . .

Intelligence must be equipped to deal with . . . [a vast] array of subjects . . . , and in the course of the years it may conceivably deal with all of the subjects at least once. It will, however, tend to deal with any single subject only when that subject is part of a threat to our national interest or is required by a prospective course of action. One of the most continuously vexing problems in the administration of intelligence is deciding which particular subjects shall be watched, reported upon, or made the object of descriptive or speculative research. Equally vexing is deciding the order of their priority. The point is that intelligence is always fully occupied, but occupied almost exclusively on a relatively few subjects of real national concern. At the same time intelligence must be ready to handle a large number of subjects.

Collecting the materials necessary to handle this large number is a task which intelligence does not do solo. Intelligence shares the task with a number of institutions— both public and private. Let me confine myself to the public ones.

Although the policy, planning, and operating officers of the federal government (both civilian and military) are the primary users (or consumers) of the finished intelligence product, they themselves are often important gatherers and producers. As men who work in the world of affairs they turn out, as by-products of their main jobs, large amounts of material which is the subject matter of strategic intelligence. The best case in point is the foreign service officer in a foreign post. His main job is representing the United States' interest in that country, but a very important by-product of his work is the informational cable, dispatch, or report which he sends in. Not merely the informational cable but the so-called "operational" cable as well. For in his capacity as US representative he must know much before he takes a stand, and he must explain much to his superiors at home when he has taken such a stand or when he asks their advice. Although the primary purpose of such communications is operational, they are frequently almost indistinguishable from those which flatly state the day's new developments. And thus the foreign service officer, although not specially trained as an intelligence man, is by virtue of his location and talent often a valuable and effective purveyor of intelligence. (For certain key parts of the world the Foreign Service does acknowledge the need for special training, and the officers which it sends to these areas may accordingly be considered intelligence officers in one sense of the word. Most of even these however will have many nonintelligence duties.)

There are others in public life, such as members of special commissions, US delegates to international conferences, traveling congressmen; and that such people make significant contributions to the total task of intelligence must be borne in mind. . . . Nor should the involuntary contributors outside of public life be forgotten: the writers, the newspapermen, the scholars, the businessmen, the travelers and big game hunters, even foreign governments themselves (in their official reports and releases) render invaluable aid. I would have no reader get the idea that intelligence—in shirt sleeves and unassisted, so-to-speak—is obliged to produce from scratch the prodigious body of data that it must have at hand. To make this point, however, in no way derogates the extremely important part of the total which intelligence itself does produce on its own hook. Some of this is confirmatory, and necessarily so; some is supplementary or complementary of that which is in; some is brand new and sufficient unto itself. Some is not merely new and vital, but is the stuff which would not, indeed could not, be turned up by any agency other than intelligence itself. All of it, plus the time and skill intelligence organizations employ in its appraisal, analysis, and tabulation, makes up the substantive content of our special category of knowledge.

THE EVOLUTION OF AMERICAN INTELLIGENCE [2]

In United States history, until after World War II, there was little official government intelligence activity except in time of combat. With the restoration of peace, intelligence organizations which the stress of battle had called forth were each time sharply reduced, and the fund of knowledge and the lessons learned from bitter experience were lost and forgotten. In each of our crises, up to Pearl Harbor, workers in intelligence have had to start in all over again.

Intelligence, especially in our earlier history, was conducted on a fairly informal basis, with only the loosest kind of organization and there is for the historian, as well as the student of intelligence, a dearth of coherent official records. Operations were often run out of a general's hat or a diplomat's pocket, so to speak. This guaranteed at the time a certain security sometimes lacking in later days when reports are filed in septuplicate or mimeographed and distributed to numerous officials often not directly concerned with the intelligence process. But it makes things rather difficult for the historian. At General Washington's headquarters Alexander Hamilton was one of the few entrusted with "developing" and reading the messages received in

[2] Chapter 3 from *The Craft of Intelligence*, by Allen Dulles, CIA director 1953-1961. Harper & Row. '63. p 29-47. Copyright © 1963 by Allen W. Dulles. Reprinted by permission of Harper & Row, Publishers, Inc.

secret inks and codes and no copies were made. Washington, who keenly appreciated the need for secrecy, kept his operations so secret that we may never have the full history of them.

To be sure, two of his intelligence officers, [Elias] Boudinot and [Benjamin] Tallmadge, later wrote their memoirs, but they were exceedingly discreet. Even forty years after the war was over, when John Jay told James Fenimore Cooper the true story of a Revolutionary spy, which the latter then used in his novel *The Spy,* Jay refused to divulge the real name of the man. Much of what we know today about intelligence in both the Revolutionary and Civil wars was only turned up many generations after these wars were over.

Intelligence costs money and agents have to be paid. Since it is the government's money which is being disbursed, even the most informal and swashbuckling general will usually put in some kind of chit for expenses incurred in the collection of information. Washington kept scrupulous records of money spent for the purchase of information. He generally advanced the money out of his own personal funds and then included the payment in the bill for all his expenses which he sent the Continental Congress. Since he itemized his expenses, we can see from his financial accountings that he spent around $17,000 on secret intelligence during the years of the Revolutionary War, a lot of money in those days. [Sir Francis] Walsingham, in England, two hundred years earlier, also kept such records, and it is from them that we have gleaned many of the details about his intelligence activities.

But the official accountings are not the only indicators that the pecuniary side of intelligence contributes to history. A singular attribute of intelligence work under war conditions is the delay between the completion of an agent's work and his being paid for it. He may be installed behind the enemy lines and may not get home until the war is over. Or the military unit that employed him may have moved hastily from the scene in victory or retreat, leaving him high and dry and without his reward. Thus it may happen that not until years later, and sometimes only when the former agent or his heirs have fallen on hard times, is a claim made against the government to collect payment for past services rendered. Secret intelligence being what it is, there may be no living witnesses and absolutely no record to support the claim. In any case, such instances have often brought to light intelligence operations of some moment in our own history that otherwise might have remained entirely unknown.

In December 1852, a certain Daniel Bryan went before a justice of the peace in Tioga County, New York, and made a deposition concerning his father, Alexander Bryan, who had died in 1825. Daniel Bryan stated that General Gates in the year 1777, just before the Battle of Saratoga, had told his father that he wished him "to go into Burgoyne's Army as a spy as he wanted at that critical moment correct information as to the heft of the artillery of the enemy, the strength and number of his artillery and if possible information as to the contemplated movements of the enemy." Bryan then "went into Burgoyne's Army where he purchased a piece of cloth for a trowsers when he went stumbling about to find a tailor and thus he soon learned the strength of the artillery and the number of the Army as near as he could estimate the same and notwithstanding that the future movements of the Enemy were kept a secret, he learned that the next day the Enemy intended to take possession of Bemis heights."

The deposition goes on to tell how Alexander Bryan got away from Burgoyne's Army and reached the American lines and General Gates in time to deliver his information, with the result that Gates was on Bemis Heights the next morning "ready to receive Burgoyne's Army." As we know, the latter was soundly trounced, an action which was followed ten days later by the surrender of Burgoyne at Saratoga. According to the deposition, Bryan was never rewarded. His sick child died during the night he was away and his wife almost died too. Gates had promised to send a physician to Bryan's family, but he had never got around to it. Seventy-five years later his son put the story on record, for reasons which are still not clear as there is no record that any claim of recompense was filed. (The original of this deposition is in the Walter Pforzheimer Collection on Intelligence Service through whose courtesy the above passages have been cited.)

Until accident or further research turns up additional information, we shall not know to what extent Gates' victorious strategy, which helped greatly to turn the tide of the war and was so instrumental in persuading the French to assist us, was based on the information which Bryan delivered. Sporadic finds of this kind can only make us wonder who all the other unsung heroes may have been who risked their lives to collect information for the American cause.

The one spy hero of the Revolution about whom every American schoolboy does know is, of course, Nathan Hale. Even Hale, however, despite his sacrifice, might have been forgotten, if his story had not been written down in 1799 by Hannah Adams in her *History of New England*. Surprising as it may now seem, twenty-two years after his death he had been entirely forgotten and, as Hannah Adams wrote, "It is scarcely known such a character existed." Apart from inspiring later generations with his fortitude and loyalty, thanks to Hannah Adams' revival of the story, Hale's misfortune had quite another significance at the time. Since Hale had been a volunteer, an amateur, mightily spurred on by patriotism but sadly equipped to carry out the dangerous work of spying, his death and the circumstances of it apparently brought home sharply to General Washington the need for more professional, more carefully prepared intelligence missions. After Hale's loss, Washington decided to organize a secret intelligence bureau and chose as one of its chiefs Major Benjamin Tallmadge, who had been a classmate and friend of Nathan Hale at Yale and therefore had an additional motive in promoting the success of his new enterprise. His close collaborator was a certain Robert Townsend.

Townsend directed one of the most fruitful and complex espionage chains that existed on the colonial side during the Revolution. At least we know of no other quite like it. Its target was the New York area, which was, of course, British headquarters. Its complexity lay not so much in its collection effort as in its communications. (. . . It is useless to collect information unless you can quickly and accurately get it to the user.)

Since the British held New York, the Hudson and the harbor area firmly under their control, it was impossible or at least highly risky to slip through their defenses to Washington in Westchester. Information from Townsend's agents in New York was therefore passed to Washington by a highly roundabout way, which for the times, however, was swift, efficient and secure. It was carried from New York to the North Shore of Long Island, thence across Long Island Sound by boat to the Connecticut shore, where Tallmadge picked it up and relayed it to Washington.

The best-known spy story of the Revolution other than that of Hale is, of course, the story of Major John André and Benedict Arnold. These two gentlemen might never have been discovered, in which case the damage to the patriot cause would have been incalculable, had it not been for Townsend and Tallmadge, who were apparently as sharp in the business of counterintelligence as they were in the collection of military information.

One account claims that during a visit André paid to a British major quartered in Townsend's house he aroused the suspicions of Townsend's sister, who overheard his conversation and reported it to her brother. Later, when André was caught making his way through the American line on a pass Arnold had issued him, a series of blunders which Tallmadge was powerless to prevent were instrumental in giving Arnold warning that he had been discovered, thus triggering his hasty and successful escape.

A typical "brief" written by Washington himself for Townsend late in 1778 mentioned among other things the following: ". . . mix as much as possible among the officers and refugees, visit the Coffee Houses, and all public places [in New York]." Washington then went on to enumerate particular targets and the information he wanted about them: "whether any works are thrown up on Harlem River, near Harlem Town, and whether Horn's Hook is fortified. If so, how many men are kept at each place and what number and what sized Cannon are in those works."

This is a model for an intelligence brief. It spells out exactly what is wanted and even tells the agent how to go about getting the information.

The actual collection of information against British headquarters in New York and Philadelphia seems to have been carried out by countless private citizens, tradesmen, booksellers, tavernkeepers and the like, who had daily contact with British officers, befriended them, listened to their conversations, masquerading as Tories in order to gain their confidence. The fact that the opposing sides were made up of people who spoke the same language, had the same heritage and differed only in political opinion made spying a different and in a sense a somewhat easier task than it is in conflicts between parties of alien nationality, language and even physical aspect. By the same token, the job of counterespionage is immensely difficult under such circumstances.

One typical unsung patriot of the time was a certain Hercules Mulligan, a New York tailor with a large British clientele. His neighbors thought him a Tory or at least a sympathizer and snubbed him and made life difficult for him. On General Washington's first morning in New York after the war was over, he stopped off rather conspicuously at Mulligan's house and, to the enormous surprise of Mulligan's neighbors, breakfasted with him. After that, the neighbors understood about Mulligan. He had obviously gleaned vital information from his talkative British military customers and managed to pass it on to the General, possibly via Townsend's network.

Intelligence during the Revolution was by no means limited to military espionage in the colonies. A fancier game of international political spying was being played for high stakes in diplomatic circles, chiefly in France where Benjamin Franklin headed an American mission whose purpose was to secure French assistance for the colonial cause. It was of the utmost importance for the British to learn how Franklin's negotiations were proceeding and what help the French were offering the colonies. How many spies surrounded Franklin and how many he himself had in England we shall probably never know. He was a careful man and he was sitting in a foreign country and he himself published little about this period of his life. However, we do know a great deal about one man who apparently succeeded in double-crossing Franklin. Or did he? That is the question.

Dr. Edward Bancroft had been born in the colonies, in Westfield, Massachusetts, but had been educated in England. He was appointed as secretary to the American commission in Paris, wormed his way into Franklin's confidence, and became his "faithful" assistant and protégé for very little pay. He successfully simulated the part of a loyal and devoted American. He was able to manage nicely on his low salary from the Americans because he was being generously subsidized by the British—"£500 down, the same amount as yearly salary and a life pension." Being privy, or so he thought, to all Franklin's secret negotiations, he was no doubt a valuable agent to the British.

He passed his messages to the British Embassy in Paris by depositing them in a bottle hidden in the hollow root of a tree in the Tuileries Gardens. They were written in secret inks between the lines of love letters. Whenever he had more information than could be fitted into the bottle, or when he needed new directives from the British, he simply paid a visit to London—with Franklin's blessing, for he persuaded Franklin that he could pick up valuable information for the Americans in London. The British obligingly supplied him with what we today call "chicken feed," misleading information prepared for the opponents' consumption. Bancroft was thus one of the first agents in our history.

To deflect possible suspicion of their agent, the British once even arrested Bancroft as he was leaving England, an action intended to impress Franklin with his bona fides and with the dangers to which his devotion to the American cause exposed him. Everything depended, of course, on the acting ability of Dr. Bancroft, which was evidently so effective that when Franklin was later presented with evidence of his duplicity he refused to believe it.

Perhaps the wily Franklin really knew of it but did not want to let on that he did. In 1777, Franklin wrote to an American lady living in France, Juliana Ritchie, who had warned him that he was surrounded with spies:

I am much oblig'd to you for your kind Attention to my Welfare in the Information you give me. I have no doubt of its being well founded. But as it is impossible to . . . prevent being watch'd by Spies, when interested People may think proper to place them for that purpose; I have long observ'd one Rule which prevents any Inconvenience from such Practices. It is simply this, to be con-

cern'd in no Affairs that I should blush to have made publick; and
to do nothing but what Spies may see and welcome. When a Man's
Actions are just and honourable, the more they are known, the
more his Reputation is increas'd and establish'd. If I was sure
therefore that my Valet de Place was a Spy, as probably he is, I
think I should not discharge him for that, if in other Respects I
lik'd him. (The original of this letter is in the collection of Franklin papers of the American Philosophical Society in Philadelphia.)

Once when the British lodged an official diplomatic protest with the French regarding the latter's support of the
American cause, they based the protest on a secret report
of Bancroft's, quoting facts and figures he had received from
Franklin and even using Bancroft's wording, a bit of a slip
that happens from time to time in the intelligence world.
Bancroft was mortally afraid that Franklin might smell a
rat and suspect him. He even had the British give him a
passport so that he could flee on a moment's notice if necessary. Franklin did express the opinion on this occasion
that "such precise information must have come from a
source very near him," but as far as we know he did nothing
else about it.

The British, also, had reason to suspect Bancroft. George
III does not seem to have fully trusted him or his reports
since he caught him out investing his ill-gotten pounds in
securities whose value would be enhanced by an American
victory.

Bancroft's duplicity was not clearly established until
1889, when certain papers in British archives pertaining to
the Revolutionary period were made public. Among them,
in a letter addressed to Lord Carmarthen, Secretary of State
for Foreign Affairs, and written in 1784, Bancroft set down
in summary form his activities as a British agent. It seems
the British Government had fallen behind in their pay-
ments to him and Bancroft was putting in a claim and re-
minding his employers of his past services. He closed with

the words: "I make no Claim beyond the permanent pension of £500 pr an. for which the Faith of Government has often been pledged; and for which I have sacrificed near eight years of my life."

Franklin's own agents in London were apparently highly placed. Early in 1778 Franklin knew the contents of a report General Cornwallis submitted in London on the American situation less than a month after Cornwallis had delivered it. The gist of the report was that the conquest of America was impossible. If Franklin's agents had penetrated the British government at this level, it is possible that they had caught wind of the intelligence Bancroft was feeding the British.

In the Civil War, even more than in the Revolution, the common heritage and language of the two parties to the conflict and the fact that many people geographically located on one side sympathized with the political aims of the other made the basic task of espionage relatively simple, while making the task of counterespionage all the more difficult. Yet the record seems to show that few highly competent continuous espionage operations, ones that can be compared in significance of achievement and technical excellence with those of the Revolution, existed on either side. No great battles were won or lost or evaded because of superior intelligence. Intelligence operations were limited for the most part to more or less localized and temporary targets. As one writer has put it, "There was probably more espionage in one year in any medieval Italian city than in the four-year War of Secession."

The reasons for this are numerous. There was no existing intelligence organization on either side at the outbreak of the war nor was there any extensive intelligence experience among our military personnel of that day. Before the Revolution, the colonial leaders had been conspiring and carrying out a limited secret war against the British for

years and by the time of open conflict had a string of active
"sources" working for them in England and moreover possessed tested techniques for functioning in secret at home.
This was not the case in the North or the South before the
Civil War. Washington was an outstandingly gifted intelligence chief. He himself directed the entire intelligence effort of the American forces, even to taking a hand personally
in its more important operations. There was no general
with a similar gift in the whole galaxy of Federal or Confederate generals. Lastly, the Civil War by its very nature
was not a war of surprises and secrets. Large lumbering
armies remained encamped in one place for long periods of
time and when they began to move word of their movements spread in advance almost automatically. Washington,
with far smaller numbers of men, could plant false information as to his strength and could move his troops so
quickly that a planned British action wouldn't find them
where they had been the day before, especially when Washington through his networks knew in advance of the British
move.

At the beginning of the Civil War the city of Washington was a sieve and the organization on the Northern side
so insecure that the size and movements of its forces were
apparent to any interested observer. It has been said that
the Confederate side never again had such good intelligence
to help them as they did at the opening Battle of Bull Run.

One of the first events of the period which apparently
pointed up the need for a secret intelligence service was the
conspiracy of a group of hotheads in Baltimore to assassinate Lincoln on the way to his first inauguration in February 1861. Allan Pinkerton, who had already achieved
some fame working as a private detective for the railroads,
had been hired by some of Lincoln's supporters to protect
him. Pinkerton got Lincoln to Washington without incident by arranging to have the presidential train pass

through Baltimore unannounced late at night. At the same time Pinkerton's operatives "penetrated" the Baltimore conspirators and kept a close watch on their activities.

Good as Pinkerton was at the job of security and counterespionage, he had little to recommend him for the work of intelligence collection except for one excellent agent, a certain Timothy Webster, who produced some good information entirely on his own in Virginia. But, unfortunately, Webster was captured early in the war, thanks to a foolish maneuver of Pinkerton, and was subsequently executed. We next find Pinkerton working directly with General McClellan on military intelligence and right in the General's headquarters. Pinkerton's idea of military intelligence was to count the noses of the opposing troops and then to count them all over again to be sure the first figure was right. Since McClellan was famous for not going into battle anyway unless he commanded overwhelming numbers, it is not likely that Pinkerton's nose-counting contributed significantly to the outcome of any battle. Even with overwhelming odds in his favor, McClellan was outmaneuvered by Lee at Antietam. When Lincoln removed him from his command after this battle, Pinkerton resigned, leaving the Union virtually without a secret service.

The fact that Lincoln had hired an agent of his own on a military intelligence mission at the time of the Battle of Bull Run did not come to light until 1876, and then, as so often is the case, it was revealed in the form of a claim against the government for reimbursement. In March of 1876, the United States Supreme Court heard a case on appeal from the United States Court of Claims in which a certain Enoch Totten brought a claim against the government "to recover compensation for services alleged to have been rendered" by a certain William A. Lloyd, "under contract with President Lincoln, made in July 1861, by which he was to proceed South and ascertain the number of troops stationed at different points in the insurrectionary States, procure plans of forts and fortifications . . . and report the facts to the President. . . . Lloyd proceeded . . . within the rebel lines, and remained there during the entire period of the war, collecting and from time to time transmitting information to the President." At the end of the war he had been paid his expenses but not the salary of $200 a month which Lincoln, according to the claim, had promised him. The case itself is interesting even with only these meager facts because of the light it casts on Lincoln's foresight at this time and the security with which he must have handled the matter throughout the four long years of the war. As the Supreme Court stated in its opinion: "Both employer and agent must have understood that the lips of the other were to be forever sealed respecting the relation of either to the matter."

Also, this case established the precedent that an intelligence agent cannot recover by court action against the government for *secret* service rendered. Said the Court: "Agents . . . must look for their compensation to the contingent fund of the department employing them, and to such allowance from it as those who dispense the fund may award. The secrecy which such contracts impose precludes any action for this enforcement." This is a warning to the agent that he had better get his money on the barrelhead at the time of his operation.

After Pinkerton left the scene, an effort was made to create a purely military intelligence organization known as the Bureau of Military Information. The responsibility for it was assigned to Major (later General) George H. Sharpe, who appears to have been a fair-to-middling bureaucrat but is not known to have conceived or mounted significant intelligence operations on his own. What did, however, bring good information to the Union was the work of occasional brave volunteers, most of whom generated their own operations and communications without good advice from any-body. One of these was Lafayette Baker, who posed as an itinerant photographer in the South and made a specialty of visiting Confederate camps in Virginia, taking pictures of the soldiers stationed in them, at the same time gathering valuable military information. He later rose to brigadier general and took charge of the National Detective Police, a sort of precursor of today's secret service. Where Pinkerton had excelled at counterespionage but had little to recommend him as an espionage operator, Baker excelled in the latter craft, but his failures as a chief of secret service lost us one of our greatest Presidents. To this day, no one knows where Baker's men were on the night of April 14, 1865, when Abraham Lincoln was sitting in an unguarded box watching a play in Ford's Theater, or why the assassins who gathered at Mrs. Suratt's boarding house, whose fanatical opinions were well known throughout Washington, were not being watched by Baker. Nor was the capture of Booth and his accomplices the work of Baker, although he took credit for it.

Elizabeth van Lew, another volunteer in the South and a resident of Richmond, stayed at her post throughout the entire war and is accounted the single most valuable spy the North ever had. Grant himself stated that she had sent the most valuable information received from Richmond during the war. In Civil War espionage any "penetration" of an important headquarters, always the most dramatic of high-level intelligence operations, is conspicuously missing, as are most of the more rewarding and devious undertakings of espionage. The closest thing to it, however, is alleged to have been achieved by Elizabeth van Lew when she procured a job for one of her Negro servants as a waitress in the house of Jefferson Davis, transmitting the intelligence this produced to Major Sharpe in Washington.

In the 1880s the first permanent peacetime military and

naval intelligence organizations were created in the United
States. The Army unit was known as the Military Information Division and came under the Adjutant General's Office. The Navy's Office of Intelligence belonged to the Bureau of Navigation. During the same decade the first US
military and naval attachés were posted to our embassies
and legations abroad, where they were to function as observers and intelligence officers. In 1903, with the creation of an
Army General Staff, the Military Information Division was
incorporated into it as the "Second Division," thus beginning the tradition of G-2, which has since remained the
designation for intelligence in the American Army. This
early G-2, however, from lack of interest and responsibility
dwindled almost to the point of disappearance, with the
result that World War I found us again without any real
intelligence service. But this time our situation was different. We were fighting abroad, the whole period during
which our troops were directly engaged lasted little over a
year, and we had allies. There was no time to develop a
full-fledged intelligence arm nor did we have to, since we
could rely largely on the British and French for military
intelligence and particularly for order of battle.

But we learned rapidly—due largely to a group of officers
to whom I wish to pay tribute. There was, first of all, Colonel Ralph H. Van Deman, who is considered by many to be
the moving force in establishing a US military intelligence.
His work is described in what I consider the best account
by an American author of intelligence services through the
ages, *The Story of Secret Service,* by Richard Wilmer
Rowan. I worked personally with Colonel Van Deman in
World War I when I was in Bern, and I can attest to the
effective work that he and his successors, General Dennis E.
Nolan and General Marlborough Churchill, did in building up the basis of our military intelligence today.

By the time the war was over, the basic framework had

been established for the various military and naval intelligence branches which continued to exist, even though in skeleton form, until the outbreak of the Second World War—G-2, CIC (Counter Intelligence Corps, which until 1942 was called the Corps of Intelligence Police) and ONI (Office of Naval Intelligence). Of equal importance was our initial experience during World War I in the field of cryptography. . . . In this area, too, a skeleton force working during the interim years of peace succeeded in developing the most vital instrument of intelligence which we possessed when we were finally swept into war again in 1941—the ability to break the Japanese diplomatic and naval codes.

It was only in World War II, and particularly after the Pearl Harbor attack, that we began to develop, side by side with our military intelligence organizations, an agency for secret intelligence collection and operations. . . . The origin of this agency was a summons by President Franklin D. Roosevelt to William J. Donovan in 1941 to come down to Washington and work on this problem.

Colonel (later Major General) Donovan was eminently qualified for the job. A distinguished lawyer, a veteran of World War I who had won the Medal of Honor, he had divided his busy life in peacetime between the law, government service and politics. He knew the world, having traveled widely. He understood people. He had a flair for the unusual and for the dangerous, tempered with judgment. In short, he had the qualities to be desired in an intelligence officer.

The Japanese sneak attack on Pearl Harbor and our entry into the war naturally stimulated the rapid growth of the OSS [Office of Strategic Services] and its intelligence operations.

It had begun, overtly, as a research and analysis organization, manned by a hand-picked group of some of the best historians and other scholars available in this country. By June 1942, the COI (Coordinator of Information), as Donovan's organization had been called at first, was renamed the Office of Strategic Services and told "to collect and analyze strategic information and to plan and operate special services."

By this time the OSS was already deep in the task of "special services," a cover designation for secret intelligence and secret operations of all kinds and character, particularly the support of various anti-Nazi underground groups behind the enemy lines and covert preparations for the invasion of North Africa.

During 1943, elements of the OSS were at work on a worldwide basis, except for Latin America, where the FBI was operating, and parts of the Far Eastern Command, which General MacArthur had already preempted.

Its guerrilla and resistance branch, modeled on the now well-publicized British Special Operations Executive (SOE) and working closely with the latter in the European Theater, had already begun to drop teams of men and women into France, Italy and Yugoslavia and in the China-Burma-India Theater of war. The key idea behind these operations was to support, train and supply already existing resistance movements or, where there were none, to organize willing partisans into effective guerrillas. The Jedburghs, as they were called, who dropped into France, and Detachment 101, the unit in Burma, were among the most famous of these groups. Later the OSS developed special units for the creation and dissemination of black propaganda, for counterespionage, and for certain sabotage and resistance tasks that required unusual talents, such as underwater demolitions or technical functions in support of regular intelligence tasks. In conjunction with all these undertakings, it had to develop its own training schools.

Toward the end of the war, as our armies swept over

Germany, it created special units for the apprehension of war criminals and the recovery of looted art treasures as well as for tracking down the movements of funds which, it was thought, the Nazi leaders would take into hiding in order to make a comeback at a later date. There was little that it did not attempt to do at some time or place between 1942 and the war's end.

When the war was over, all but the secret intelligence branch and the analysis branch of the OSS was dissolved. Even these for a time threatened to disappear.

For a short time after V-J Day, it looked as though the United States would gradually withdraw its troops from Europe and the Far East. This would probably have included the disbanding of intelligence operations. In fact, it seemed likely at the end of 1945 that we would do what we did after World War I—fold our tents and go back to business-as-usual. But this time, in contrast to 1919 when we repudiated the League of Nations, we became a charter member of the United Nations and gave it our support in hopes that it would grow up to be the keeper of world peace.

If the Communists had not overreached themselves, our government might well have been disposed to leave the responsibility for keeping the peace more and more to the United Nations. In fact, at Yalta Stalin asked President Roosevelt how long we expected to keep our troops in Europe. The President answered, not more than two years. In view of the events that took place in rapid succession during the postwar years, it is clear that in the period between 1945 and 1950 Premier Stalin and Mao Tse-tung decided that they would not wait for us to retire gracefully from Europe and Asia; they would kick us out.

Moscow installed Communist regimes in Poland, Rumania and Bulgaria before the ink was dry on the agreements signed at Yalta and Potsdam. The Kremlin threatened

Iran in 1946, and followed this in rapid succession by imposing a Communist regime on Hungary, activating the civil war in Greece, staging the takeover of Czechoslovakia and instituting the Berlin blockade. Later, in 1950, Mao joined Stalin to mastermind the attack on South Korea. Meanwhile, Mao had been consolidating his position on the mainland of China. These blows in different parts of the world aroused our leaders to the need for a worldwide intelligence system. We were, without fully realizing it, witnessing the first stages of a master plan to shatter the societies of Europe and Asia and isolate the United States, and eventually to take over the entire world. What we were coming to realize, however, was the need to learn a great deal more than we knew about the secret plans of the Kremlin to advance the frontiers of communism.

In his address to Congress on March 12, 1947, President Truman declared that the security of the country was threatened by Communist actions and stated that it would be our policy "to help free peoples to maintain their free institutions and their national integrity against aggressive movements seeking to impose on them totalitarian regimes." He added that we could not allow changes in the status quo brought about by "coercion or by such subterfuges as political infiltration," in violation of the United Nations Charter.

It was by then obvious that the United Nations, shackled by the Soviet veto, could not play the role of policeman. It was also clear that we had a long period of crisis ahead of us. Under these conditions, a series of measures were taken by the government to transform our words into action. One of the earliest was the reorganization of our national defense structure, which provided for the unification of the military services under a Secretary of Defense and the creation of the National Security Council.

At that time President Truman, basing his action upon

a blueprint that General Donovan had submitted, recommended that a central intelligence agency be created as a permanent agency of government. A Republican Congress agreed and, with complete bipartisan approval, the CIA was established in the National Security Act of 1947. [For further discussion see "Why the CIA Was Created," below.—Ed.] It was an openly acknowledged arm of the executive branch of government, although, of course, it had many duties of a secret nature. President Truman saw to it that the new agency was equipped to support our government's effort to meet Communist tactics of "coercion, subterfuge, and political infiltration." Much of the know-how and some of the personnel of the OSS were taken over by the Central Intelligence Agency. Fortunately many ranking officers of the OSS had remained in the various interim intelligence units which had functioned under the aegis of the State and War departments in the period 1945–47.

The CIA, however, was not patterned wholly either on the OSS or on the structural plan of earlier or contemporary intelligence organizations of other countries. Its broad scheme was in a sense unique in that it combined under one leadership the overt task of intelligence analysis and coordination with the work of secret intelligence operations of . . . various types. . . . Also, the new organization was intended to fill the gaps in our existing intelligence structure without displacing or unduly competing with other existing US intelligence units in the departments of State and Defense. At the same time, it was realized that the State Department, largely dependent for its information on the reports from diplomatic establishments abroad, and the armed forces, dependent mainly on its attachés and its military installations abroad, could neither be expected to collect intelligence on all those parts of the world that were becoming increasingly difficult of access nor to groom a standing force of trained intelligence officers. For this reason, CIA was given the mandate to develop its own secret collection arm, which was to be quite distinct from that part of the organization that had been set up to assemble and evaluate intelligence from other parts of the government.

One of the unique features of CIA was that its evaluation and coordinating side was to treat the intelligence produced by its clandestine arm in the same fashion that information from other government agencies was treated. Another feature of CIA's structure, which did not come about all at once but was the result of gradual mergers which experience showed to be practical and efficient, was the incorporation of all clandestine activities under one roof and one management. Traditionally, intelligence services have kept espionage and counterespionage in separate compartments and all activities belonging in the category of political or psychological warfare in still another compartment. CIA abandoned this kind of compartmentalization, which so often leads to neither the right hand nor the left knowing what the other is doing.

The most recent development in American intelligence has been a unification of the management of the various intelligence branches of the armed forces. In August 1961, the Defense Intelligence Agency (DIA) was established under a directive issued by the Department of Defense. An outstanding Air Force officer, Lieutenant General Joseph F. Carroll was named as its first director. . . . DIA was not a merger of the intelligence branches of the armed services, but primarily an attempt to achieve maximum coordination and efficiency in the intelligence processes of the three services.

Thus, in contrast to our custom in the past of letting the intelligence function die when the war was over, it has been allowed to grow to meet the ever-widening and more complex responsibilities of the time. The formation of such agencies as the DIA, like the earlier creation of CIA itself, is the result of studied effort to give intelligence its proper stature in our national security structure. There is, of course, always the possibility that two such powerful and well-financed agencies as CIA and DIA will become rivals and competitors. Some of this could be healthy; too much of it could be both expensive and dangerous. A clear definition of functions is always a requisite and this, in broad outlines, exists. Furthermore, the high caliber of the officers, military and civilian, directing the two agencies, if maintained, should guarantee effective performance, but it is vital to protect the authority of the Director of Central Intelligence over the estimating functions of our intelligence work.

WHY THE CIA WAS CREATED [3]

Any government, including even those which have the most elementary international association, must collect foreign intelligence. This pursuit of a special kind of information—and its refined product, which is knowledge—is an indispensable function.

Vigorous nations depend on their leaders to devise a strategy that will provide both for their security and for their economic and political well-being. History teaches us that leaders cannot meet this responsibility unless they learn the political, economic and military capabilities and intentions of other nations.

Today, great nations are armed as never before. And the leaders of great states must take heed of the risk involved. Furthermore, in their economic life, nations both large and small are interdependent, one with the other—more now than ever before in the past.

[3] Excerpt from "Why We Need the CIA," article by John A. McCone, CIA director 1961-1965. *TV Guide.* v 24 no 2:6-9. Ja. 10, '76. Reprinted by permission of the author. © 1976 Triangle Publications, Inc.

On the military side, the maneuvering of possible hostile forces, the deployment of mass-destruction weapons and —what could be of greater importance?—the hidden development of even more advanced weaponry, must all be discovered in good time and their possible effects measured. On the economic side, the task of intelligence services that provide information to safeguard the well-being of the state has lately been vastly amplified: a consortia has appeared that seeks to get economic advantage by imposing quotas and exorbitant prices on raw materials that heretofore have been in relatively free international flow.

Walter Lippmann [political journalist] once wrote, "Foreign policy is the shield of the Republic"; and Sherman Kent, the distinguished historian, has said, "Strategic intelligence is the thing that gets the shield to the proper place at the right time. It is also the thing that stands ready to guide the sword." [See "Intelligence Is Knowledge," above.]

What these men are saying is merely that sound decisions designed to protect the security interests and the economic and political welfare of our country can only be made against a background of knowledge. Without the knowledge gained from foreign-intelligence gathering methods, and the appraisal of the significance of that knowledge developed through careful and studious analysis of the information, leaders can make no policy decisions with reasonable assurance that the action they plan is a correct one.

All vigorous nations, large and small, support a foreign-intelligence apparatus. Invariably, the organization is clandestine. Even in open societies, practical considerations demand that the organization be kept out of public view and its work made known only to the few who need to know. Usually, the authority granted to this organization and the control over it are both embedded at the topmost echelon of power. When you make public disclosure of the intimate details of a foreign-intelligence service you paralyze an otherwise effective operation.

It is no surprise that the so-called superpowers—the United States and the Soviet Union—both maintain elaborate intelligence systems; but the intelligence efforts of other countries throughout the world, some forty in all, are also significant. Among them all, the intelligence service of the United States is the only one (except West Germany's) that was initiated and authorized legislatively—in our case, by congressional action after long and thoughtful consideration by both houses of the Congress and with its operations and budgets reviewed by congressional committees.

How Did We Get Into the Foreign Intelligence Business?

We got into the foreign intelligence business fairly recently. Between the two world wars, the United States maintained little in the way of an intelligence community. To be sure, the Army and the Navy maintained separate intelligence units of their own, specifically to meet their needs in times of war. The Department of State kept a watchful eye on world happenings, and ambassadors regularly reported their observations. But, we had no organization in existence to analyze the whole flow of information and to study the dangers to American security inherent in the pattern of action reported from abroad. Thus, an inquiry into our surprise at Pearl Harbor, conducted after World War II, disclosed that our various government agencies had in hand—days prior to the actual attack—all essential information concerning Japan's preparations for war, including the assembly and departure of the Japanese fleet. The State, War and Navy departments had each gathered the information, and each had used it for its own special interests, but—disastrously—no branch of government then had the duty to put the information *together* and alert the President of impending danger.

It was to correct this gaping deficiency in our government machinery that the Central Intelligence Agency was created under the National Security Act of 1947. To ensure that it would remain apart from partisan attachments and parochial interests, the CIA was developed essentially as a civilian organization.

It was then recognized that many departments of government must, in the interests of their departmental responsibilities and to broaden the base of all intelligence appraisals, continue their own intelligence efforts. I am speaking of the intelligence division of the State Department known as the Bureau of Intelligence and Research—a thoughtful organization that assesses information for the State Department; the Defense Intelligence Agency that supports the Secretary of Defense and the Joint Chiefs of Staff, coordinates the work of the three separate service intelligence units and manages the corps of military attaches; the intelligence units of the army, navy and air force maintained to serve their chiefs of service and to provide current technical intelligence information to field commanders; the intelligence units of the Treasury Department, and the Energy Research and Development Agency (formerly the Atomic Energy Commission), both of which contribute important specialized information on foreign developments; and, finally, the Federal Bureau of Investigation, which, in the course of its extensive domestic operations, is constantly unearthing information either originating abroad or having a significant foreign connection.

At the apex of this large, complex community is the Central Intelligence Agency. Its director, as the President's principal intelligence officer, is charged by presidential directive with the responsibility for the general direction of the community as a whole. This function he carries out in his individual role and as chairman of the United States Intelligence Board, which is the senior body of the community, and is composed of the directors of several departmental intelligence organizations.

The Central Intelligence Agency's responsibilities, as established by law, range from the collection of overt and covert intelligence by its own considerable establishment to the correlation and assessment of intelligence findings from all sources. In addition, the CIA is charged with protecting intelligence sources and methods and with executing tasks assigned by the President or the National Security Council. Under this latter mandate fall such essential activities as counterintelligence, which means ferreting out, together with the FBI, the covert activities of others. Also, the mandate covers covert political action and covert paramilitary operations—the supporting or training and equipping of third-country nationals who espouse our principles of freedom and who are under attack by Communist forces directed from the center of Communist power.

Sources of Intelligence

Unevaluated intelligence—raw, as it is known in the trade—comes in many ways. Through the long sweep of history, human contact, both open and covert, has been the major source of intelligence. Conversations between heads of state, reports from ambassadors and military attaches, and articles in newspapers and other publications all contribute to the inventory of information. But the richest source is usually the secret agent, a well-trained professional, concealed under disarming cover, who usually moves in the highest and most informed circles.

The ethics of clandestine intelligence operations have long been debated and some would do away with them. The fact is that no international covenant forbids clandestine operations, and they go on as they have for centuries. At least forty nations today support clandestine services—no great state can abandon them.

In the recent past, technology has enormously lengthened the reach and sharpened the penetration of intelligence. High-flying aircraft carrying sophisticated cameras, supplemented by orbital satellites equipped with even more advanced cameras, have been able to look down into fortress societies and record in startling detail what is actually developing.

A correspondingly wide range of electronic sensing and tracking devices makes it quite possible to accurately deduce the yield of nuclear devices, exploded either in the atmosphere or underground, at great distances; and to supply information on the characteristics and performance of military equipment that is being developed and tested beyond otherwise impenetrable frontiers. Indeed, in the event of a surprise attack, we would get our first warning of the blow being prepared from these intelligence-gathering systems.

Analysis and Evaluation

Gathering the information is only the start of the intelligence process. The raw material, once obtained, must be drawn together, analyzed and correlated. And it must be evaluated before it becomes useful knowledge. An estimate of the developing situation emerges, and from this estimate a head of state, consulting with his advisers, can chart a course of action that will best meet the developing situation. Without the intelligence itself and the sophisticated estimate, the head of a government would be groping toward a decision.

All raw intelligence entering the community flows in one form or another to the CIA. From this processing comes a digest of what it all means and an estimate of what its consequences could be. The bits and pieces of information from near and far are studied by men and women of the highest capabilities: political scientists, economists, historians, linguists, engineers, physicists and other experts.

Daily intelligence reports are sent to the President and his principal advisers. Finally, there appears a body of papers known as the National Intelligence Estimates, presenting a continuing analysis of military, political and economic situations that bear directly on our national security and well-being. All are the product of the analytical process and are prepared within the halls of the Central Intelligence Agency, with a substantial oversight by the United States Intelligence Board.

Preparing this body of literature in its various forms is, in my opinion, the most important activity of the agency. It is certainly the least publicized.

In the discharge of its duties, the United States Intelligence Board gathers weekly at CIA headquarters—and often more frequently—to review the national estimates prepared by the CIA analysis. This review is made before the estimates are passed to the President and to others by the director. It is also within the board's purview to advise the director on how best to supply the intelligence needs of the nation's policymakers, schedule the flights of the reconnaissance satellites and photographic planes, fix the tasks of the National Security Agency, advise the precautions that may be desirable for protecting the nation's intelligence sources and methods, and maintaining a watch office to be constantly on the alert for surprise hostile developments. [The National Security Agency was established in 1952 by presidential directive and combined in 1972 with the Central Security Service established in accordance with a presidential memorandum. The combined missions of the combined

Agency/Service are communications security and foreign intelligence information production.—Ed.]

CIA'S STATUTORY FUNCTIONS [4]

In the National Security Act of 1947 the CIA was assigned five specific functions, to be performed under the direction of the National Security Council. This unique status of CIA should be noted. In the formal structure it reports directly to the National Security Council as an advisory agency to the President, who is chairman of NSC. CIA's statutory functions are as follows:

1. To *advise the National Security Council* on intelligence matters of the government related to national security

2. To make recommendations to the National Security Council for *coordination of intelligence activities* of departments and agencies of government

3. To *correlate and evaluate* intelligence and provide for its appropriate dissemination within the government

4. To perform for the benefit of existing intelligence agencies such *additional services* as the NSC determines can be efficiently accomplished by a central organization

5. To perform *other functions and duties* relating to national security intelligence as the National Security Council may direct

Such functions are prescribed in what is often called an *organic act,* in that the responsibilities and functions of the agency are defined only in a general way, with more precise assignment of functions left to presidential and NSC directives. But it is noteworthy that Congress intended that all

[4] Excerpt from Chapter IV of *The Intelligence Establishment*, by Harry Howe Ransom. Harvard University Press. '70. p. 85-7. Reprinted by permission of the publishers from *The Intelligence Establishment* by Harry Howe Ransom, Cambridge, Mass.: Harvard University Press, Copyright © 1970 by the President and Fellows of Harvard College. The author, a professor of political science at Vanderbilt University, was formerly research associate in the Defense Studies Program at Harvard.

of CIA's statutory basic functions should be related to or of benefit to the *intelligence* function. Only by seriously distorting the meaning of the term *intelligence* is it possible to find statutory justification for the wide range of strategic services that CIA actually has come to perform. Such services can only be justified by stretching the meaning of the term, admittedly a common practice. This apparently has been done. By a more strict definition of intelligence, it can be argued that CIA performs functions, which over the years have cost billions of dollars, that have never been specifically authorized by Congress.

There are a number of significant *provisos* included in the statute establishing CIA:

1. The CIA shall have no police, subpoena, law-enforcement powers or internal security functions. Here Congress intended to allay the fears of some Americans that a *Gestapo* or *KGB* would be created in the guise of central intelligence, and, incidentally, perhaps to quiet any FBI concern over the presence of a rival in the internal security field. [The *Gestapo* was the secret police force of the German Nazi state, notorious for its terrorism and atrocities. The *KGB* is the Russian Committee of State Security concerned mainly with internal security.—Ed.]

2. It is made especially clear that CIA should not supersede most departmental intelligence functions, for the act states that the several departments shall "continue to collect, evaluate, correlate and disseminate departmental intelligence."

3. The 1947 Act further gave the director of Central Intelligence, subject to presidential and NSC recommendation and approval, the right to inspect the intelligence product of all government security agencies and specifies that these agencies will make their intelligence available to CIA for "correlation, evaluation and dissemination." One exception is the jealously guarded province of the FBI, the

vast files of which may be approached only upon "written request."

The CIA is managed by a director and deputy director, both appointed by the President, subject to confirmation by the Senate. Commissioned officers of the armed services, whether in active or retired status, are eligible for either appointment. The two positions, however, may not be occupied simultaneously by officers of the armed services. Allen Dulles became the first civilian to be named director when appointed early in the first Eisenhower Administration (1953).

A revision of the CIA statute in 1949 by the Central Intelligence Agency Act was designed to improve CIA administration by strengthening the powers of the director. This new statute gave him virtually free rein to hire and fire without regard for Civil Service regulations.

The 1949 Act also exempts CIA from the provisions of any laws requiring publication or disclosure of the "organization, functions, names, official titles, salaries or numbers of personnel employed." The Bureau of the Budget is directed to make no reports to Congress on these matters.

Perhaps even more important, the director of Central Intelligence can spend funds from his multimillion-dollar annual appropriation on his personal voucher. This may occur "for objects of a confidential, extraordinary, or emergency nature." This is truly an extraordinary power for the head of an Executive agency with thousands of employees and annual expenditures in the hundreds of millions of dollars. The agency also is permitted to purchase or contract for "supplies or services" without advertising; to contract for "special research or instruction of agency personnel" at private universities; to make special travel allowances and "related expenses" for intelligence agents on overseas assignment; and to approve the entry of up to one hundred aliens into the United States in the interest of foreign intelligence activities. An amendment to the Act in 1951 authorized the CIA to employ up to fifteen retired officers of the armed services, allowing such officers to receive either their retirement pay or CIA compensation. Several more recent amendments provide for other special "fringe benefits" for intelligence personnel. About one half of the total funds expended by CIA is audited in routine fashion by the General Accounting Office. The remainder, including the "unvouchered funds," are considered to be so secret that they are audited by a special supersecure procedure established for this purpose. Intelligence officials insist, however, that such funds are audited just as stringently as more open ones.

II. AMERICAN INTELLIGENCE: WHERE IT WENT WRONG

EDITOR'S INTRODUCTION

The now famous 1972 break-in at Democratic party headquarters in the Watergate complex initiated congressional probes into a broad range of government activities—investigations that eventually exposed, among other matters, irresponsible and illegal operations on the part of the nation's intelligence establishment. The issues—even the activities—involved were hardly new to experienced observers of the scene. What was new was that the Congress and the press "discovered" an issue that had been too complex and politically volatile to address previously.

The misuse of the nation's foreign (and domestic) intelligence structure had been justified principally on the basis of "national security," and, perhaps more to the point, the historical privilege of the presidency. Although the actual episode of the Watergate break-in turned out to have had nothing to do with national intelligence interests or activities, the fact that the participants had been formerly associated with the CIA forced open the door that had been closed to previous inquiries. Eventually both the philosophy and the operations of the CIA and the other government intelligence organizations—National Security Agency (NSA), Federal Bureau of Investigation (FBI), Defense Intelligence Agency (DIA)—were investigated by congressional committees and by President Gerald R. Ford after the resignation of Richard M. Nixon.

With the disclosure of the irregularities and illegalities of covert American intelligence activity at home and abroad, the press felt free to discuss what many journalists had already known for some time. Much of what appeared in print about US intelligence activities was the product of sensationalism and inadequate research. Fortunately, however, the length of the investigations provided an adequate period of coverage to allow for serious and informed commentary to come to the fore.

This section includes some of the most informative writing. It opens with an excerpt from Professor Harry Howe Ransom's *The Intelligence Establishment* analyzing the problem at CIA. Published well before the revelations of Watergate in 1973, this analysis reveals the extent to which detailed information about the nature and structure of the US intelligence establishment was easily available. Professor Ransom holds that "governmental confusion about intelligence relates and contributes to . . . [the] problem of defining organizational purpose. Organizations and functions of government should not be justified or evaluated in their own terms; they must be related to purpose." Three selections from the New York *Times* follow: Anthony Lewis discusses President Ford's plan for solving the intelligence problem and concludes that it "cries out for congressional attention"; Tom Wicker comments on the public reaction to the disclosures; Nicholas M. Horrock points up the fact that some in Congress knew for many years what was going on.

The presentation continues with a *Wall Street Journal* editorial holding that the focus of the discussion is on the wrong problem—that it should be not on "dirty tricks" and the centralizing of controls but on keeping the analysis of intelligence decentralized and as independent as possible. Then, Lord Chalfont, a British foreign affairs expert and former intelligence officer, pointing up the need for intelligence operations in our modern world and the problems inherent in such activities, questions the reasons behind the current one-sided revelations of names of individuals connected with espionage.

The section ends with an article by Sidney Hook, emeritus professor of philosophy at New York University and senior fellow at Hoover Institution on War, Revolution and Peace at Stanford University. His thesis is that "we must maintain intelligent intelligence operations" with a full awareness of the fact that "silence, secrecy, and a choice among evils are dictated by public as well as by personal morality."

THE "CIA PROBLEM" [1]

Scandal is the word best characterizing the context in which most citizens have viewed, in recent times, the intelligence establishment, particularly the CIA. The problems and scandals that have beset the intelligence system are the result of entanglements of definitions, purpose, organization, and policy. An overlay of mythology further beclouds the subject. Perhaps the best way to symbolize this mythology is to cite the observation by Trevor-Roper [H. R. Trevor-Roper, noted British historian] that in the popular mind the chief of a contemporary intelligence system is seen as a "superspy." In reality he is a bureaucrat. He works within a political system, and his office is the locus of great potential influence.

The heart of the definitional problem is that "intelligence" has come to be used as a term to label two disparate activities: information gathering and secret political action. This semantic confusion is so pervasive that it extends into

[1] Chapter X from *The Intelligence Establishment,* by Harry Howe Ransom. Harvard University Press. '70. p 235-54. Reprinted by permission of the publishers, from *The Intelligence Establishment* by Harry Howe Ransom, Cambridge, Mass.: Harvard University Press, Copyright © 1970 by the President and Fellows of Harvard College. The author, a professor in the political science department at Vanderbilt University, was formerly research associate in the Defense Studies Program at Harvard.

the highest levels of government and obfuscates conceptual —and thus organizational—clarity on the subject. A simpler way of saying this is that the government does not always know what it is doing in the "intelligence" field. If so, officials do not in reality control intelligence operations. This allows intelligence men to exert an undue, and often unseen, influence on policy.

Governmental confusion about intelligence relates and contributes to the additional problem of defining organizational purpose. Organizations and functions of government should not be justified or evaluated in their own terms; they must be related to purpose. Intelligence activities sometimes are undertaken for no other reason, it would seem, than that an intelligence apparatus stands by, awaiting an assignment. And much of the time both the "purpose" of a mission and the information on which it has been planned are secret and cannot be publicly discussed. Indeed, in some instances purpose and mission are not even discussed in high government councils because of "security."

Purpose in turn relates to organization. A principal technique of secret intelligence is the use of "cover," the pretense that something is what it is not. Possibly there is a relation between the widespread use of "cover" and the absence of conceptual and organizational clarity. For example, a commercial airline pretends to be privately operated when it is in fact a government airline, secretly sponsored. The CIA has become more than an intelligence agency because not only does it operate airlines, "free" radio stations, and phony foundations, but it is also engaged in underground political action and psychological warfare in foreign areas. It can be found directing undeclared wars in distant lands, oblivious to international law, the "rules of war," or the Geneva Conventions. Also it has penetrated deeply into American domestic institutions. This multiplicity of roles blurs conceptual thinking about the intelligence system and about relating organization to purpose.

This ambivalence, in turn, affects policy, for policy comes to be formulated in the midst of conceptual and semantic confusion. The results are likely to be inefficient, sometimes even counterproductive. But such inefficiency will be difficult to recognize because the criteria for evaluation are confused, if they exist at all. One enters, therefore, the realm of Alice in Wonderland, where confusion is compounded by definitional and conceptual caprice. Efficiency is difficult to judge for the further reason that "intelligence activities" in their countless forms are so compartmental . . . that the total picture is never visible; measures of efficiency are difficult to devise and to apply.

One might hypothesize a symposium of two dozen of the best-informed men in the United States on the subject of intelligence activities. Their communication would be hampered to some degree by isolated compartments of knowledge, definitional confusion, and differing "images" about the nature of an intelligence system. . . . Public information and understanding are even more severely obscured by these limitations. Much more than other aspects of government and politics, then, intelligence systems defy controlled observation and full understanding. Consequently, they may also defy the policy controls implicit in a democratic system.

Stereotypes of the Intelligence System

A number of competing images, or stereotypes, about intelligence activities have emerged from the mélange of fiction and half-truth and from the fact that espionage and associated activities are now a major international industry.

One among the prevalent stereotypes depicts the world's second oldest profession as resembling a vintage Marx Brothers movie. In this view intelligence activities involve a lot of adventuresome, slapstick activity, adding up to very little. There appear to be large numbers of those who believe, or pretend to believe, that intelligence activities are little more than something to be joked about; not to be taken seriously.

A more pervasive stereotype is a second one, casting the spy or secret agent in the role of the suave superman, conducting his business with British manners, a cool efficiency, and ruthless power to obtain his objective. It could be argued that these stereotypes have only broad cultural impact and do not affect the serious business of state policy or international relations. But consider the fact that Adolf Hitler and his henchman Heinrich Himmler had been readers of "novelettes" about the exploits of the British Secret Service which they apparently came to believe were instrumental in the creation of the British world empire. Misled by a set of fiction-based illusions, Hitler determined to have a secret service of the "British kind" to help him gain his empire. His hopes of a "gigantic, ubiquitous, infallible, secret service, like the British Secret Service of his imagination," according to Hugh Trevor-Roper, were never fulfilled. But the whole world was profoundly affected by these, among others, of Hitler's illusions.

Still a third view of the subject depicts the world of espionage populated by the small-minded, sadistic policeman, dealing in the back alleys of world politics with chiselers or mentally unstable ideologues. Thus the picture is that of an espionage system populated by a group of small-time international racketeers.

As in most stereotypes, there is an element of truth in each of these. Stereotypes aside, one may view secret intelligence and political action as a growing international industry, profoundly influenced by technology and organized now into high government bureaucracies capable, by their activities, of either causing or preventing trouble in a dynamic international political arena.

Terminological confusion is compounded by designating as "intelligence operations" actions that more accurately should be called secret political intervention. This confusion is institutionalized in the United States, as earlier explained, by housing two disparate functions, intelligence and secret political operations, under the same CIA roof.

Interventionism Added to Intelligence Role

In 1947 Allen Dulles wrote that "intelligence work in time of peace differs fundamentally from that in time of war." Since that time, Americans have become increasingly aware that distinctions between war and peace have become blurred. Since the Korean war a consensus has developed that national security required the indefinite maintenance of a military establishment, designed both for deterrence and "flexible response." The collapse of the World War II alliance with Russia and its dissolution into an ideological-power conflict between the United States and the Soviet Union, created the cold war. The American objective became the "containment" of Soviet power, which meant that the United States had to develop an organization within the intelligence system to counter subversion, and to wage or to counter various forms of psychological warfare. These activities would supplement the intelligence, that is to say informational, needs generated by an upward-spiraling arms race.

To sustain a strategy of containment sometimes-by-intervention has required decision making founded on carefully developed forecasts of what is likely to happen in the future or estimates of what can be made to happen. Demands upon the central intelligence system have, consequently, continued to increase.

While playing the role of "sentinel-on-duty"—a product of the "Pearl Harbor complex"—the intelligence system has the opportunity of shaping the "pictures in the mind" of the nation's decision makers. The fact that the intelligence apparatus has been given the operational functions of underground foreign political action and psychological warfare has further compounded the "CIA problem." It has become a problem of such dimensions that one observer wrote in 1968 that, excepting Vietnam actions, "nothing the US Government had done in recent years in the field of foreign policy has created so much controversy as its intelligence operations, especially the secret subsidizing of private American institutions." (W. J. Barnds. Intelligence and Foreign Policy: Dilemmas of a Democracy. *Foreign Affairs,* Jan. 1969. p 281.)

A Storm of Bad Publicity

In trying to meet America's global commitments, the CIA came to be assigned roles far beyond the intent of Congress in 1947 when it created the CIA as part of the National Security Council. From the start, definitional confusions and organizational entanglements characterized the missions of this "most peculiar agency." Prior to 1960, however, the CIA generally received a "good press." For the most part, Americans knew little of what the agency's functions were, or what it had achieved. Its apparent failures—to anticipate, for example, the onset of the Korean war, to predict Soviet attainment of nuclear power, or in the Middle East crisis of 1956—were not highly publicized. Such "failures," moreover, could be interpreted as deficiencies in the *use* of information by policymakers as much as in the provision of accurate estimates.

The 1960s proved to be the CIA's decade of degradation. Publicized trouble began with the U-2 affair in May 1960, on the eve of a carefully planned summit meeting with the Soviet Union. While the U-2 is now generally regarded as a notable technical achievement in intelligence gathering, the government's handling of the U-2 episode raised widespread criticism of policy, professionalism, organization, and control. Moreover, the incident dramatized the inherent incompatibility of diplomacy and espionage. This was followed, in 1961, by the Bay of Pigs invasion, which raised even more penetrating questions about the CIA—this time from some of its former supporters. The press dropped its critical restraint in writing about the agency and published all information that could be obtained. For the first time the CIA and its leadership became "cover story" material in the mass media.

The destruction of the intelligence ship U.S.S. Liberty in the June 1967 Arab-Israeli war, with the loss of thirty-four American lives, and the North Korean capture of a similar ship, the U.S.S. Pueblo, and its crew in 1968, followed later by the loss of a Navy espionage aircraft, dramatized to the public some of the costly risks intelligence agencies were taking. Perhaps most perplexing of all were the disclosures early in 1967 that the CIA had been secretly subsidizing, for more than fifteen years, several dozens of American private institutions, to support various overseas programs of those organizations (New York *Times*, Feb.-Mar. 1967). Another major shock to public sensitivities came in the summer of 1969, when through a murky picture of charge and countercharge, fact and allegation, it appeared that the CIA was involved, while collaborating with Army Special Forces "Green Berets," in political assassinations in Vietnam. Disclosures such as these caused some persons to wonder where the distinctions lay between our own and totalitarian systems.

Where Did the CIA Go Wrong?

The sentiments and confusions of many Americans, even before the increasing number of disclosures, were perhaps best expressed by . . . [the late] President Truman: "There is something about the way the CIA has been functioning that is casting a shadow over our historic position, and I feel that we need to correct it." (Washington *Post,* Dec. 22, 1963) Since Truman wrote in 1963, the CIA has remained the uncorrected problem child of American foreign policy. From Vietnam to Czechoslovakia, from the Congo to the "Green Berets" disclosures, American secret agents continue to leave the impression with many persons at home and abroad that they do more harm than good. Our adversaries laugh at CIA and claim that the letters stand for "Caught in the Act." Our friends abroad, however, are frightened. One writer in the British publication, the *New Statesman* (Sept. 3, 1965), for example, saw America "dangerously near conducting international relations through a secret police all but completely independent of elected authority." Too many others have the same view, even if rarely based upon adequately detailed knowledge. Where did the CIA go wrong?

A few weeks before his death, President John F. Kennedy denied in a press conference that CIA was operating overseas independently. Referring to Vietnam, he stated bluntly that CIA was operating "under my instructions." Although Kennedy had voted for a joint congressional committee on intelligence in the unsuccessful Senate move in 1956, as President he no longer favored such a proposal. He was, he said, "well satisfied" with existing controls. His true concern, however, is revealed by the fact that shortly before he died he was in process of creating a task force to survey the global intelligence and other secret operational activities of the United States, to improve coordination and efficiency. Perhaps, too, he was concerned with the quality of information from Vietnam where, as we now know, the lives of so many have been sacrificed to the ignorance of so few. As in most previous studies, however, the intelligence community was investigating itself. The three-man task force initiated by President Kennedy represented only the State Department, the Pentagon, and the CIA. It remained for President Johnson to receive the report, and no publicity was given it. Doubts and misgivings have remained, not only about the coordination, but about policy control and the competence of the CIA and other intelligence agencies. No major organizational changes, however, were visible to outsiders following that study, other than semiofficial intimations that the CIA's budgets had been reduced in the years since the Bay of Pigs.

Trauma Over Secret CIA Subsidies

Perhaps the greatest dismay and trauma over the activities of CIA came with disclosures of the agency's vast program of secret subsidies. Early in 1967, the public and Congress learned something of the scope of the agency's involvement with private domestic organizations. Prior to these disclosures, a very limited amount of public knowledge existed about CIA's special links since 1952 with some private foundations, university research centers, book publishers, labor and cultural organizations. But the scope of such programs and specific details were well-kept secrets until February 1967, when *Ramparts* magazine (Mar. 1967) disclosed the specifics of CIA's financing, for nearly fifteen years, of the overseas programs of the National Student Association, a student-managed organization comprising more than three hundred member colleges and universities in the United States. Between 1952 and 1967, it was later learned, the NSA received more than $3 million in CIA secret funds for its international programs. In one year, more than three fourths of NSA's total budget was from the CIA, supplied through "front" and "conduit" foundations. Moreover, the NSA headquarters building in Washington, D.C., was subsidized by mortgage payments from the CIA. Funds were provided primarily so that the United

States could be "properly" represented by college students at various international youth conferences abroad, in which the Communist movement was strongly represented. Such projects were organized under the CIA's division for Psychological, Political, and Paramilitary programs (PPPM). Money was provided also by PPPM to allow the initiation and promotion of non-Communist youth organizations in some of the developing nations. Similar subsidies, it became known, were supplied by CIA to dozens of other private American organizations, including academic, labor, church, legal, and literary groups, for their overseas programs. Defenders of such programs argued that they were necessary expedients in the psychological warfare of cold war; that the Communists had to be fought with their own weapons.

Reactions to these revelations varied widely. There were demands for congressional investigations and for a reorganization of the CIA. Some critics proposed CIA's abolition. Many of its defenders were willing to admit that the publicity had further damaged the agency's image and had created serious complications for American students and researchers working overseas. CIA's supporters were quick to note that such programs resulted from policies made at the highest levels under every President since Truman. The CIA, it was argued, had not undertaken secret subsidization "on its own," as some seemed to believe. One of CIA's harshest critics, Walter Lippmann, acknowledged the need for a Central Intelligence Agency but would sharply limit its role to foreign information gathering. Not since the crisis over the Bay of Pigs in 1961 had the agency been involved in so much public controversy. Vice President Humphrey declared he was not at all happy about the CIA. Senator Richard Russell of Georgia, Chairman of the Senate's "watchdog" subcommittee on the CIA and long its defender from congressional critics, urged reforms in the system.

Responding to the congressional, editorial, and public

criticism, President Johnson ordered CIA financing of the National Students Association to be ended. On February 15, 1967, he named a three-man committee to review the secret subsidy programs. Under Secretary of State Nicholas Katzenbach was appointed chairman; others serving were John Gardner, secretary of Health, Education and Welfare, and Richard Helms, director of Central Intelligence. Perhaps to assure access to crucial facts, the CIA always is represented on bodies charged with investigating the agency—a questionable arrangement. A public version of the committee's report was issued on March 29, 1967, accompanied by a presidential statement accepting its findings. President Johnson promised to consider the recommendation "that the government should promptly develop and establish a public-private mechanism to provide public funds openly for overseas activities." Toward this end, he appointed Secretary of State Dean Rusk to head an eighteen-member committee comprising public and private representatives, including one college student, to make more detailed recommendations for alternative means of subsidizing certain foreign operations.

The Katzenbach Committee recommended, and the President accepted, a policy statement stipulating that "no federal agency shall provide any covert financial assistance or support, direct or indirect, to any of the nation's educational or private voluntary organizations." Any existing support was to be terminated, in most cases by the end of 1967. Future exceptions to such a policy might be permissible "only where overriding national security interests so require," and on specific approval by the secretaries of State and Defense. But the committee's most pointed reference to the whole scandal was, in effect, an admission of wrongdoing in the past, to wit: "In no event should any future exception be approved which involves any educational, philanthropic, or cultural organization." Alternatives to secret subsidies awaited the report of the Rusk Committee, and any subsequent congressional action. The committee has rendered no public report, nor had Congress taken any action well into 1969.

The most profound political and moral problems have been raised by the secret subsidy disclosures. A university or organization which only pretends to be open, or whose true means of support is falsified, raises fundamental questions about leadership judgment. Such camouflage can poison the academic wells, just as it can spoil open access for the American professor innocently seeking data in scholarly research overseas. The Center for International Studies at MIT, for example, was at its founding financed in part by the Central Intelligence Agency. But its links to CIA were not publicly revealed in 1951-1952, when this secret support was initiated. Recall ironically, that for a number of years in which the research center at MIT received secret CIA funds, the institution's president, Dr. James Killian, served as chairman of a special presidential board designed to provide public, nongovernmental surveillance of the CIA and related agencies. It could be argued that MIT was in one sense providing "cover" for CIA. This kind of arrangement was ultimately abandoned by MIT, yet suspicions continuing into the present were generated about other academic research institutes which then or now may have provided "cover."

One of the greatest dangers of the cold war mentality is that it tends to ape the adversary. Certainly our scholars, books, foundations, universities, and others in the private sector ought to remain free of the suspicion that they are available for use as "cover" by secret agencies. The US Government, at the end of 1967, announced that it had discontinued all secret subsidies to private voluntary institutions in the United States. Some alternative means of governmental support will be required for those overseas projects that serve both American ideals and the national interest. The form of subsidy used, and the CIA as the disbursing agency, are unacceptable for the future, for they represent a step toward a totalitarian society. The waters of American free institutions have already been muddied by these ill-advised experiments of 1947-1967. It would be hard to demonstrate that the national security would have been seriously endangered had such programs not been undertaken. It is somewhat easier to demonstrate that the American free society has been injured by what was done.

A few headlines from the New York *Times* point to one aspect of the damage done: "Asia Foundation Banned by India" (February 16, 1968); "Mexican Theories on Unrest Blame Both C.I.A. and the Reds" (October 14, 1968); "Iraqi Public Links the C.I.A. to Coup" (July 28, 1968); "Italian Premier Backed on [C.I.A.] Intelligence Scandal" (February 2, 1968); "Passer of Che's Diary, Due to Return to Bolivia, Pledges Disclosures on C.I.A." (August 17, 1968); and "Iraq Executes 4 as Spies for C.I.A." (April 14, 1969). Most significant, from the domestic point of view, is the fact that since 1966 CIA recruiters have been unable to hold scheduled interviews on the campuses of a number of American universities because of student protest and, in some cases, because of actual violence. The point is less the question of domestic protest, and more the fact that what is being protested is a supposedly secret activity of government.

Many have asked, "What is the danger; what's wrong with this?" One answer has been given by Professor Henry Steele Commager in testimony before the Senate Committee on Foreign Relations, February 20, 1967. The danger of the secret subsidy, he said,

is that it substitutes the immediate advantage for the long run disadvantage; that it uses great things like scholarship, science, the community of learning, truth, for immediate purposes, which it doubtless thinks are worthy, but which, in the long run, are not to be compared with the larger purposes of learning, scholarship, literature, art, and truth.

Put more simply, why destroy what you are trying to protect?

Problems of Policy, Organization, and Control

As of . . . [1970], fundamental organizational changes have continued to be resisted by the leadership of the intelligence community. Clearly lacking since 1955 has been a thoroughgoing inquiry of the "Hoover Commission" type into the government's total intelligence system, including covert operations overseas. Such a nonpartisan inquiry, parts of which would necessarily proceed in secret, ought to be made at least every five years.

Focus of such an inquiry would be the major agencies, including the CIA, the Pentagon's Defense Intelligence Agency, the National Security Agency, and the Department of State. One of its investigative tasks would be to take a close look at the sponsorship of research by these agencies and by such organizations as the Agency for International Development, the armed services, the Arms Control and Disarmament Agency, and others.

The problems which would be surveyed by such an inquiry center upon issues of organization, policy control, "cover," and secrecy. (See *New Republic,* Dec. 11, 1965. pp 12-15.)

Organization. Is the intelligence establishment properly organized? There is strength in the argument that espionage, counterespionage, and clandestine political action overseas need to be under unified direction and control. But it is of questionable validity to combine these activities with the massive research-and-analysis performed by the CIA and continue to call the organization an intelligence agency. This combination of research and analysis intelligence work with covert political action and psychological warfare has made it patently impossible to maintain secrecy for that which ought to be secret; has made it difficult to recruit high-quality personnel for research and analysis; and has prompted serious duplication and conflict in some overseas operations. Not only has a large and possibly duplicating Defense Intelligence Agency grown up in the Pentagon, but the FBI is sometimes tempted to reassert its claim for an overseas intelligence role, at least in Latin America, where it had extensive World War II experience.

The Central Intelligence Agency ought to be divided so that the branch for covert operations is separated from that for research and analysis. The aim of such a division of functions would be (1) to disentangle the organization that produces "finished intelligence" from that which carries out operations, sometimes based crucially upon the evaluated information supplied; (2) to bring back some respectability to the CIA—a respectability that has gradually diminished with the increased public knowledge that one of its arms is essentially a "Department of Dirty Tricks," a fact that has caused much alienation between the intellectual community and the intelligence system; (3) to diminish the vulnerability of the CIA to critics at home and abroad who commonly characterize the agency as a sinister force in foreign affairs; (4) and, finally, to enable the truly secret branch of government to preserve such secrecy more effectively.

The arguments in favor of separating the dual functions of the CIA are more persuasive than a number of counterarguments frequently put forth by defenders of the organizational status quo: (1) that secret agents and analysts can benefit from a close organizational proximity; (2) that the ability of CIA to gain generous appropriations from Congress would be sharply reduced if the glamourous "action" arm were removed from its jurisdiction; (3) that serious problems would be raised about the role of the director of

Central Intelligence if the two major functions were separated; and (4) that there is no other feasible place to assign the covert operations of government which now use the CIA, in effect, for "cover."

The most generalized and persuasive argument for radical change is that the present system has not worked; it has tended to be self-defeating. The CIA has become a foreign policy liability, and its status at home remains under a serious and debilitating cloud of suspicion.

Control. Is CIA controlled adequately at the highest governmental level? As just noted, there are difficult problems about where best to place the intelligence and secret operations functions within the policy making structure. But the most serious question involves the control by responsible political authority of espionage, counterespionage, and political warfare overseas. No foreign secret action should be undertaken until after the most careful weighing of risks against possible gains, and particularly a careful and realistic analysis of the prospects for secrecy and the consequences of public exposure. The State Department, acting for the President, or the President himself, should have a meaningful veto in this regard.

Beyond a certain point the secret agent, whether spy, secret propagandist, or guerrilla warrior cannot be controlled. To set loose expensive networks of secret agents is to open a Pandora's box of potential blunders, misfortunes, and uncontrollable events. To pack off a secret agent with a satchel of money to intervene, say, in a Brazilian election, and expect to maintain tight operational control of him is a dubious expectation. Failure to understand this may in part explain the lack of effective coordination and control that characterized some secret operations under the Eisenhower Administration. Under Kennedy, there was a promise of stronger presidential coordination and leadership in foreign affairs. Yet the Bay of Pigs, the greatest public disaster to befall the CIA, revealed continuing weaknesses in foreign operational concept, command, and control. The State Department remained in the shadows, failing to exercise its proper authority, while the Pentagon and CIA were in the forefront, playing an ill-defined but patently decisive role. As Theodore Sorensen recalls, Kennedy felt that State had a "built-in inertia which deadened initiative and that its tendency towards excessive delay obscured determination." A question never adequately explored is the extent to which CIA activism may have been a consequence of State Department inactivity. There is little visible evidence that these problems have been of serious concern to either the Johnson or Nixon Administration.

Defenders of the secret intelligence system are quick to insist that there has always been an elaborate set of policy controls on all secret operations. Some have argued that intelligence and other secret operations are perhaps the most tightly controlled activities in all of government.

One cannot examine the evidence on this point, but experienced former officials of the intelligence system argue, sometimes persuasively, that CIA officials have always been required to seek and gain prior approval from policymakers before initiating any secret operations. In the earliest days of the system, procedures for approving secret operations were less formal than in more recent years. Even in recent times, however, it would seem that programs, once initially approved, were rarely given intensive scrutiny, particularly when the question of their continuation came up for policy review. The U-2 incident and more recently the Pueblo case are examples of dangerous routinization of operations.

Since the early years of the Eisenhower Administration, which established elaborate procedures for all kinds of national security decisions, covert political activities have been reviewed and approved (or rejected) by a group representing the highest levels of government: the President's special assistant for national security affairs, the Number Two man in the Pentagon and in the State Department, and the director of Central Intelligence. This group has been called at various times the "54-12 Group," "Special Group," and more recently the "303 Group." Other supervisory groups have existed for the review of more technical intelligence operations. Forms and procedures for policy review and control have always existed; CIA leaders have never felt that they were free to operate "on their own." Even before special projects or secret operations come to the highest level for review (if the "303 Group" so recommends, the matter can be passed directly to the President's desk), proposals have run the gamut of interdepartmental review at the lower administrative echelons, perhaps at the level of the assistant secretary or even of the "country desk." Ambassadors in the countries involved theoretically, as of 1969, have a veto under normal circumstances, in any proposed secret operations within their jurisdiction.

When hundreds of secret operations are projected by a nation with worldwide commitments and extensive operational forces, true control will be determined by three factors: (1) the basic assumptions or "state of mind" of those at the highest policy levels; (2) the intelligence they possess, which is mainly supplied by the same system they are supposed to be controlling; and (3) the energy and determination of top policymakers to make this control effective. One may seriously doubt whether their "span of attention"—given a vast array of other duties and of decisions they must make—can actually result in effective policy control. And, further, it should be kept in mind that operational management of a secret agent may be at once the most important and most difficult to exercise. Control, as it has existed through much of CIA's history, has perhaps been more a matter of form than actuality. At any rate, the results have been less than the nation should demand.

Cover. Secret warriors and intelligence agents depend heavily upon "the art of cover," as they term it. They must often shield their true identity, purpose, and operations. As noted earlier, World War II had produced a vast international apparatus for applying American power around the world, including an Office of Stategic Services. When the war ended, its director, General [William J.] Donovan, proposed that the secret part of this apparatus be made permanent. [See "The Evolution of American Intelligence," in Section I, above.] According to Donovan's assistant, Robert H. Alcorn, in referring to the OSS director's postwar plan:

> We were everywhere already, he argued, and it was only wisdom and good policy to dig in, quietly and efficiently, for the long pull. Overseas branches of large corporations, the expanding business picture, the rebuilding of war areas, government programs for economic, social and health aid to foreign lands, all these were made to order for the infiltration of espionage agents. (*No More Vietnams;* ed. by R. M. Pfeffer. Harper & Row. 1968. p 66.)

And so the CIA took advantage of numerous opportunities for "cover" in the postwar years. And espionage, after the Truman Doctrine, was easily transferred to political action.

The CIA and the higher level "controllers" have shown themselves to be inadequately sensitive to issues raised by such activity. One example of how far CIA has gone in the infiltration of other American overseas agencies for the purpose of "cover" is to attempt to make use of the Peace Corps. In the corps' formative days, a determined effort was required to forestall CIA infiltration attempts. With a few possible exceptions, the threat was successfully resisted, but it is astounding that the CIA threat existed at all, particularly in the face of Communist claims that the Peace Corps was no more than an espionage front.

Use of legitimate agencies for intelligence cover is a traditional gambit of almost all governments. But how far should CIA be allowed to go in using for cover the diplomatic service, foreign economic aid missions, including university-operated technical assistance missions in foreign countries, and other agencies? The answer is: not as far as they have gone. Even more serious are the questions raised by CIA's invasion of the domestic private sector, its secret use of foundations, universities, publishers, and others for the agency's purposes. Most universities undertaking government-financed defense research have done so openly, although some of the work done might remain "classified." A healthy shift of university policy away from secret research in recent years indicates that important basic values of scholarly independence are being reasserted.

Secrecy. The CIA director is responsible "for protecting intelligence sources and methods from unauthorized disclosure." Even with secrecy oaths, binding after employment with the agency, lie-detector tests as commonplace personnel routine, and "top secret" labels profusely applied, the CIA has been patently unsuccessful in keeping its proper secrets. To combine research and analysis with covert strategic services requires a blanket of secrecy over the entire agency. The blanket has proved to be riddled with holes. One important reason for this has been a lack of respect among journalists, on Capitol Hill, and in other branches of government for the agency's efficiency and the validity and propriety of some of its operations. Another reason may be Allen Dulles's lack of a passion for anonymity while CIA chief, particularly during President Eisenhower's Administration. While head of CIA, Dulles made more than sixty major public addresses on a variety of foreign policy topics. More recent directors, John McCone, Admiral William F. Raborn, and Richard Helms, have, commendably, gone about their job more quietly.

The disclosure in 1965 by Prime Minister Yew of Singapore that a CIA agent had been involved in a $3 million bribe attempt to cover up an unsuccessful CIA effort to penetrate Singapore's intelligence service is a case in point. An enormous risk of disclosure was involved as compared with any possible gain. Another example of confusion in CIA, this time on the home front, was a CIA press conference in January 1964, at which CIA spokesmen gave their estimates of Soviet economic growth rates to demonstrate that Russia was falling behind her own expectations. The agency unwisely had entered the policy sphere. It was, at best, doing the job of (a) the White House, (b) the State Department, or (c) the nation's propaganda agency.

Role of the Press

No public press in recent history has been as full of details about its government's secret services as that in the United States. In Great Britain, an open society, as we have seen, the press cooperates with proper governmental requests for secrecy. In a closed society like the Soviet Union or China, disclosure of state secrets by the mass media is never a problem.

Time was when the American press exercised considerable restraint in publishing information about intelligence activities. Prior to 1960, important segments of the American press knew of U-2 aircraft overflights of the Soviet Union (as did the Soviet government) but refrained from disclosure. And prior to the Bay of Pigs disaster in 1961, James Reston reports that newsmen knew "all about" the Kennedy Administration's plan, but some withheld the information. In retrospect, Kennedy told the then managing editor of the New York *Times* that he wished the press had disclosed much more information than it had revealed about the plan. This he suggested, might have forced cancellation of a patently bad plan. Significantly, the President held this view only in retrospect. (James Reston. *The Artillery of the Press*. Harper & Row. 1967. pp 21, 30-1.)

So it is debatable whether press disclosures about CIA activities have from the agency's point of view been a liability or an asset. On the liability side, some have argued, as has William J. Barnds, that these "disclosures have created a public awareness that the US Government has, at least at times, resorted to covert operations in inappropriate situations, failed to maintain secrecy, and failed to review ongoing operations adequately. The public revelation of these weaknesses, even though they are now [1969] partially corrected, hampers CIA (and the US Government) by limiting those willing to cooperate with it and increasing [the number of] those opposed to it and its activities." (W. J. Barnds. Intelligence and Foreign Policy: Dilemmas of a Democracy. *Foreign Affairs,* Jan. 1969. p 292.)

From the public's point of view, it can be argued that the press leadership is as competent to judge the national interest as any government group. The press can, and probably will, show restraint—even self-censorship—when this is seen to be in the national interest and if the press maintains confidence in the competence and good judgment of the government in its planning and conduct of secret operations. These are indeed big "ifs," and rarely is there unanimity on foreign policy issues. But most important of all, a secret operation, if justified, should only be planned and authorized by highest authority, and then only if chances of maintaining secrecy are strong enough to justify the risks of disclosure. If not, some other instrument of policy should be chosen, or no action taken. There are, of course, no formulas for easy decision-making.

Another problem involves the posture to be taken by the government if "caught in the act" of a secret operation. In the past, US officials have issued denials which on occasion have caused acute embarrassment when the charge was proved by evidence, as in the case of the U-2 aircraft downed within the Soviet Union. The policy of most governments in these situations is to refuse any comment on the matter. This would seem to be the wisest policy for the American government to follow in the future, along with a very conservative attitude toward mounting secret operations in the first place.

The foregoing pages have described . . . the American government's organizational response to the worldwide information explosion and to the shifting requirements of the nation's world power position. I have chosen to apply to the variety of intelligence organizations the descriptive term *intelligence establishment.* By this I have not meant to suggest a monolithic "invisible government" but a set of agencies with common missions and great potential power in shaping the picture of the external environment in the decision maker's mind. I do not pretend to have found a way to measure this power but I see it existing and growing, often in league with a military-industrial-labor complex. And thus the problem grows of controlling these new loci of power, for uncontrolled political power is incompatible with democratic government.

Finally, to summarize my prescription: (a) organizational mistakes which have combined foreign-information gathering and political action need to be repaired by surgery; (b) covert political operations should only be undertaken to prevent a direct threat to national security and as an alternative to overt military action; and (c) the President and State Department should exert effective policy control over secret foreign operations at all times. Put another way, the President and National Security Council must effectuate their authority to know what the intelligence establishment is doing and to control it.

Can Man Survive Technology?

Paradoxically, intelligence, in both its principal meanings, will be required if man is to survive technology. An intelligence establishment is both a threat and a possible savior to any nation's legitimate political system. It is a threat in an age of information explosion, when policymakers must depend heavily upon the system to collect, analyze and interpret, and communicate information, often at great speed. Thus the intelligence establishment possesses the power potentially to control the informational assumptions of a decision. Intelligence is a possible savior because correct decisions for the future cannot be expected, barring luck, to result from inadequate information. A decision rarely can be better than the information upon which it is based. But the required information is not likely to be forthcoming in the absence of a clearly defined purpose, supplemented by rational information policies, strategies, and organizations.

The threat of a gargantuan intelligence establishment can best be contained by an alert press, and by vigilance on the part of Congress, the public, and the scholar about what will certainly be a continuing problem. And the promise of an intelligence system is intimately related to an acknowledgement of its dangers and closer attention than previously given to its proper policy, organization, and control.

LAWS, MEN, AND THE CIA [2]

The CIA activities brought to light during . . . [1975]—domestic spying, assassination plots and the rest—troubled many Americans as not only immoral but illegal. It concerned people, it frightened them, that a powerful secret agency seemingly operated in large areas without any authority in law.

For example, the National Security Act of 1947, the

[2] Article by Anthony Lewis, journalist and author, staff reporter of the New York *Times*. New York *Times*. p 25. F. 23, '76. © 1976 by The New York Times Company. Reprinted by permission.

CIA's basic charter [see article "CIA's Statutory Function," in Section I, above], had been generally understood to bar it from any domestic activities. Yet the Rockefeller Commission [on CIA Activities within the United States] found that the agency had run a massive domestic probe of antiwar groups, Operation Chaos, that "unlawfully exceeded the CIA's statutory authority."

Seen against that background, President Ford's intelligence reorganization plan is disturbing. For it does not try to establish a clear basis in law—in statutes—for what the intelligence agencies can and cannot do. It leaves most of the controls to executive orders, and it even purports to authorize . . . some things that had been considered unlawful.

Mr. Ford's order says that foreign intelligence agencies generally may not operate inside the country. But then follows a long list of exceptions.

One exception is that the agencies may conduct "physical surveillance" of present or former employees, or employees of contracting firms, to stop unauthorized disclosure of "national security information." In other words, the CIA can spy on a former official to keep him from disclosing that the United States is running a secret war in Laos or intervening in Angola.

Another exception indicates that the CIA may on occasion examine Americans' tax returns. Another allows it to infiltrate organizations in this country if they are made up largely of foreigners and are "reasonably believed to be acting on behalf of a foreign power." Another allows collection of corporate information when it "constitutes foreign intelligence or counterintelligence."

Now it may be that some or all of those things have to be done. But is it clear that they should be done by our foreign intelligence agencies rather than by a domestic police organization?

[Also to be considered] is whether the CIA should—or

can be given such powers by executive order. This is not just a narrow question of law. It is a fundamental question of constitutional legitimacy.

In the American system of government, the exercise of power must always be linked to some authority in law. We do not, like the British, put our faith in individuals and unwritten traditions; we believe in formal rules and institutions.

When President Truman seized the nation's steel mills to stop a strike during the Korean war, the Supreme Court reflected a deep public instinct in deciding that such a step went beyond any "inherent powers" of the President. Similarly here, political wisdom as well as the Constitution counsels that President Ford go to Congress for legislation. Otherwise he will appear to be saying that the way to deal with intelligence illegalities is to declare them legal.

What the intelligence community needs above all is to restore the public confidence that has broken down. The legislative process, whatever its faults, is a powerful way to build consensus in this country. An order imposed suddenly by a President, without public debate, and subject to sudden change by future Presidents, is never going to restore a sense of legitimacy.

It is just as important to establish rules of law for covert action abroad as for the domestic side. Relying on "inherent powers" of the President for legal authority, as Mr. Ford has done, is too uncertain and too dangerous. There has been real doubt that the 1947 act authorized any covert action aside from intelligence-gathering. Those doubts can only be settled, and legitimacy established, by carefully drawn legislative limits.

Legitimacy should also be an aim in planning oversight of the CIA and the other agencies. That the Executive should scrutinize its own operations is fine, but experience has shown the foolishness of relying entirely on any institution to police itself, especially when shielded from public scrutiny.

As a major reform after the Bay of Pigs, President Kennedy reconstituted the President's Foreign Intelligence Advisory Board. It failed utterly to stop abuses and illegalities. Now President Ford has appointed a new oversight board: three private citizens, average age just under seventy, who will be available part-time. Pollyanna would have trouble finding any hope in that.

In sum, the Ford intelligence plan cried out for congressional attention. [See article "Senate Select Committee Report," in section III, below.] The Senate, at least, appears likely to set up a meaningful oversight committee. That committee should have jurisdiction over intelligence budgets: the key to making the Executive listen. And its first duty should be to start through the legislative process the laws by which the intelligence community will live.

THE DARK AT THE TOP [3]

The outlines were generally known but still it was hard to credit the details disclosed in Washington about the Central Intelligence Agency's plots to assassinate foreign leaders and the Federal Bureau of Investigation's efforts to assassinate the character and career of the Rev. Martin Luther King.

In fact, if Dr. King was right in believing that the FBI was trying to drive him to suicide—and documentary evidence appears to support that interpretation—then the bureau can be said to have tried to assassinate him physically. Its method was only slightly more devious than the CIA's poisons and its deals with Mafia killers.

[3] Article by Tom Wicker, journalist and author, staff reporter of the New York *Times*. New York *Times*. sec IV, p 17. N. 23, '75. © 1975 by The New York Times Company. Reprinted by permission.

Can these things actually have been done in the name of the American people, by their authorized security agencies, through the consent or indifference of their elected political leaders? The answer is yes, and that fact has to be faced in all its implications before anything effective can be done to prevent such obscene actions in the future.

The Senate intelligence committee, for example, is going to offer legislation to outlaw assassination plots against foreign leaders. But what good will that do if nothing else is done? Both CIA and FBI officials have shown themselves repeatedly willing to ignore and break the law. Even the committee's own report tells how a former CIA official, Richard Bissell, waived aside suggestions that planning to kill Patrice Lumumba [former Congolese premier who was murdered by tribesmen in 1961] might be legally a murder plot; and Richard Helms, the former CIA director and . . . [former] ambassador to Iran [whose resignation was accepted in November 1976—Ed.] told the committee himself that it had never occurred to him to check on the agency's legal authority for the mail intercepts it used in snooping on American citizens.

But the intelligence committee is centering its recommendations on greatly improved congressional oversight, including a joint House-Senate oversight committee. Here again, the intention is good, but if nothing else is done little will be changed in the actual operations of the FBI, the CIA and other security agencies. They have shown time and again their ability to co-opt or to dupe their congressional overseers, not to mention their supposed political masters in the Executive branch; and a major reason why they so frequently disclose their great desire for more formal oversight arrangements is that they know such committees as that now being proposed usually become the ardent defenders and proponents of the agencies supposedly being overseen and controlled.

The more important necessity, without which oversight is likely to be futile, is for Congress to rewrite and sharply restrict the missions of the security agencies to clearly defined activities. The open-ended authority the CIA now has to do virtually anything either directed by the National Security Council or not specifically prohibited by it is one root of its troubles. Another probably is the linkage between its intelligence-gathering and analysis function, and its covert operations.

Not all covert operations are bad—for example, the clandestine organization of democratic labor unions in third world countries where there might otherwise be no such unions—but to vest the power to conduct them in a huge secret agency which also provides the government's basic intelligence estimates gives that agency too much power to influence rather than serve foreign policy. And the very scope of the CIA's mission now insures that it can usually find some justification and necessity—not to mention means—for doing almost anything it thinks useful to "national security."

Somewhat similarly, the FBI's sweeping authority to conduct counterespionage operations gave it the opening to engage in domestic political spying; since American Communists or Fascists or dissidents might become foreign agents, they had to be watched and reported on, in the bureau's view. And Congress itself, by requiring such abominations as the "security register" of Americans to be arrested and confined in the event of a war, gave the bureau an even broader mandate to check up on the political views and activities of thousands of citizens.

But oversight, new laws and more restricted missions still will not "control" the security agencies unless the example is set for them at the top, in Congress and the Executive branch. Who stood up to, and demanded accountability from J. Edgar Hoover in his prime? In fact, when

President Johnson and Congress combined to exempt him from mandatory retirement in 1965, they gave him license to pursue his own peculiar version of "national security"—including his war on Martin Luther King, which became known *at the time* both in the White House and Congress.

As for the CIA, if its efforts to murder Fidel Castro and Patrice Lumumba were not actually ordered by President Kennedy, the agency still drew its impressions of what was desirable and permissible in no small part from the political atmosphere in which it operated. More than any other factor, that atmosphere, in the Executive branch and Congress, determines finally whether oversight and the law will prevail or become ciphers.

A FEW IN CONGRESS COULD SEE WHAT THE SPOOKS WERE DOING [4]

On January 22, 1975, the former director of Central Intelligence [1966-1973], Richard Helms, sat before the members of the Senate Foreign Relations Committee in their ornate meeting room just below the main Senate chamber.

It was not a comfortable session for the urbane, intelligence-officer-turned-ambassador (to Iran). [Helms' resignation from his post as ambassador to Iran was accepted by the President on November 4, 1976.—Ed.] He had testified before this committee in 1973 and events and disclosures since have contradicted what he told them.

I would like to say the way I guided myself during the six and one half years I was director [he said at one point]. I made up my mind that I wasn't going to lie to any congressional committees, that I was going to be forthcoming as I thought I could under the circumstances existing at the hearing, whether I was before an oversight committee or someplace else, and I must say I always had the alternative of going to the senator privately and say please will you pull back on that, we are getting into a very sensitive area. . . .

[4] Article by Nicholas M. Horrock, Washington correspondent of the New York *Times*. New York *Times*. p 1. F. 1, '76. © 1976 by The New York Times Company. Reprinted by permission.

Whether Mr. Helms was indeed as forthcoming with congressional committees as he should have been is now under investigation by the Department of Justice.

But his account of the methodology of relations with congressional committees is instructive on why congressional oversight apparently failed so completely. In the current public debate, congressmen and senators flatly claim the intelligence community lied to them, misled them or kept them in the dark about its unseemly activities, and its failures.

The agency's men, Mr. Helms, and his successor William E. Colby, just as flatly contend that over the years they found a Congress that was often disinterested and as often unwilling to listen because it didn't want to get involved.

The congressional investigations of the past year, however, have turned up substantial evidence that between these simple extremes the intelligence agencies ran virtually scot free of control for a mixture of reasons.

Elitism

One, Senator Frank Church [Democrat, Idaho] has suggested in interviews, was "elitism." The four small committees (two in the House and two in the Senate) that had the responsibility of watching the intelligence agency and another four that had nominal control over the Federal Bureau of Investigation were an elite.

Even within the committee memberships, there was an elite and the accountability of the intelligence agencies was not to the committees as a whole, but to their chairmen, for instance Senator John Stennis, the Mississippi Democrat who chaired the Senate Armed Services Committee or Senator John McClellan, the Arkansas Democrat who heads the Intelligence subcommittee of the Senate Appropriations Committee.

At no time prior to 1975, when the congressional

investigations opened and a new law required that the President brief the foreign relations committees on covert operations, did more than two dozen of the 535 members of the Senate and the House have any real inside knowledge of secret Agency activities or the inner workings of the Bureau. This elite included the oversight committee chairmen and a few select Capitol Hill personages, the kind of men that former Director J. Edgar Hoover characterized as friends of the Bureau. Some had entree on some issues and others on other matters. No single congressman knew everything.

Both the Agency and the Bureau chose their confidants for their power and their sympathy and they chose carefully. Senators Stuart Symington [Democrat, Missouri] and Henry Jackson [Democrat, Washington] were the kind of men who enjoyed the friendship and confidence of top intelligence officers. It was to Mr. Jackson that Agency officials went in 1973 in an effort to block Senate investigation of their Chile operations. Mr. Helms sought out both senators to air his problems about testifying on Watergate and Chile.

As Mr. Helms adroitly suggested in his testimony, these private relationships could blunt an over-inquisitive committee or senator. The private conversation of gentlemen was certainly preferable to sworn testimony of a committee inquisition, even one conducted behind closed doors.

It permitted the Agency to report on its own terms, purge itself of the responsibility to have told Congress—even if the telling was in a Georgetown salon or a private office.

If the report was unpleasant or embarrassing, the Agency men could faithfully promise that it would not happen again and the congressman could absolve them. There was, one former Agency official wryly suggests, a little of the Roman Catholic confessional in the whole procedure.

The Nedzi Case

Representative Lucien Nedzi, a Detroit Democrat, found himself in this position in the spring of 1973. The Agency had just completed an internal inquiry, the Inspector General's report, that was to later become the basis for the investigations of 1975. Mr. Nedzi, who had recently come to head a House oversight committee, was briefed by William Colby. He was told about domestic surveillance, burglaries and assassination plots. He was also assured that it would never happen again.

Mr. Nedzi chose not to tell any members of his committee and indeed his secret knowledge was not known to Congress until . . . press accounts compelled him to confirm it.

It goes without saying that on many occasions, men in Congress didn't want to know too much. Part of the desire not to know, particularly to have prior knowledge, was based upon a practical political reason. If a senator or a congressman knows about a covert operation ahead of time, does not protest it and it fails, he shares some of the responsibility. When the Bay of Pigs operation failed in 1961, there was no claim for authorship credit.

In the January 22 hearing with Mr. Helms, Senator Hubert H. Humphrey [Democrat, Minnesota] anguished out loud about his reservations:

I have very mixed feelings about this. I just put a note down here "Do we want the C.I.A. to tell us what they have been doing in some countries?" Because I think some of these things are a good deal cheaper than the Bay of Pigs. There are so many countries in which these covert activities take place that I think there is a real general policy question whether we ought to have them or not. If we do, how much do we want to know about them and who are we going to trust with the information?

Presumably Mr. Humphrey, through both his more recent committee responsibility and his service as Vice President to Lyndon B. Johnson, knows more than the average United States senator does about the nation's covert operations.

There are practical reasons that details of national security programs are not spread around government.

The more people who know a secret, the less of a secret it is. But there are some new influences pressing for responsible congressional oversight which are worth noting. Intelligence Agency and Bureau of Investigation men themselves have learned the unhappy feeling of being left out on a limb. One former intelligence operative has speculated that they want someone to "share the heat," particularly "when the heat was applied fifteen years later."

WRONG PROBLEM AT THE CIA [5]

Given the type of attention that has been focused on the Central Intelligence Agency over the last year or so, it has been predictable enough that efforts at "reform" would center on greater centralization of the intelligence function. No type of reform could do more harm.

The attention has defined "the CIA problem" as "dirty tricks." This problem has been real enough, and a tighter scrutiny of covert operations is clearly in order. The committee supervising such operations ought not to authorize them without holding a real meeting, for example. No doubt the attention and debate will sensitize officials to the danger of excesses, and a committee specifically charged with oversight is a prudent idea. But beyond that, proposals to solve the dirty-tricks problem are bound to have a certain cosmetic quality.

This is because no one has any solution. Aside from a

[5] Editorial reprinted from *Wall Street Journal*. p 18 (3-Star Eastern edition). F. 24, '76. Reprinted with permission of the *Wall Street Journal* © 1976 Dow Jones & Company, Inc. All Rights Reserved.

few newspaper columnists still rioting against Vietnam, no one really wants to outlaw all covert operations. And no one has any very good suggestions about which to outlaw and which to sanction. The truth is that there is no way to program a computer to make such decisions; some things still must be left to the judgment of responsible officials. No doubt they have made and will make mistakes, but taken as a whole the revelations of the last year do not lead us to believe that the dirty-tricks problem is a crisis for American society, or even the chief problem of the intelligence services.

Yet in trying to frame cosmetic solutions to this problem, nothing is more natural than to centralize. The notion is that dirty tricks result from loose controls, and can be prevented by more centralized control. Thus the main feature of President Ford's reforms is to give the director of Central Intelligence "resource control" over all intelligence services, or in other words, budget authority over not only the CIA but intelligence functions in the Pentagon and elsewhere. [New York Democratic Representative] Otis Pike's House Select Committee on Intelligence has proposed going even further, entirely abolishing the Defense Intelligence Agency. [See article "Outrage Turns to Indifference," in Section III, below.]

Representative Pike's committee ought to read its own report. At least in the version leaked and now in the public domain, it is in many ways a sloppy and shallow report, but it does show some sense of the real problem. It notes, for example, that covert operations "have been forced on a reluctant CIA." It concludes, "All evidence in hand suggests that the CIA, far from being out of control, has been utterly responsive to the instructions of the President and the Assistant to the President for National Security Affairs."

Even more importantly, the Pike Committee report provides plenty of evidence that such responsiveness by various

intelligence agencies extends not merely to covert operations, but to the shaping of intelligence itself. In Vietnam,
for example, "pressure from policy making officials to produce positive intelligence indicators reinforced erroneous
assessment of allied progress and enemy capabilities." On
the current dispute over possible Soviet violations of the
strategic arms agreements, similarly, it remarks on "Dr.
Kissinger, with his passion for secrecy and his efforts to consolidate ultimate control of important intelligence functions, through his various bureaucratic roles."

This, not dirty tricks, is the classical problem of intelligence. In debating what later proved to be deliberate
German violations of the naval disarmament treaties in
1935, Winston Churchill complained, "somewhere between
the Intelligence Service and the ministerial chief there has
been some watering down or whittling down of the facts."
Prime Minister Baldwin defended his policies by explaining
that in any event rearmament was not politically realistic,
especially since the pacifist issue had just cost the government the by-election at Fulham.

Intelligence indicators are always murky and subject to
different interpretations, after all, and intelligence commu-
nities are by nature inbred. The danger is that what will
prevail in the murk, consciously or not, are subtle pressures
for conformity and above all the political needs of policymakers to win public support for their policies or simply to
get past the next election.

This problem can never be wholly solved, but clearly it
will be exacerbated by abolishing some of the present intelligence agencies, or even by centralizing the budget control crucial in any bureaucracy. Quite the contrary, the real
solution to the problem of the CIA would concentrate on
ways to keep the analysis of intelligence decentralized and
as independent as possible.

ARE THE "SPOOK-SPOTTERS" REALLY ENRAGED AT ESPIONAGE? [6]

It was during the war that a Foreign Office official, walking along Whitehall [in London], was accosted by a stranger who asked him which side the War Office was on. "Ours, I hope," he replied courteously, and passed on.

I was reminded, in a somewhat bitter way, of this pleasantly inconsequential story by the recent campaign in which the names and addresses of alleged intelligence agents have been published in books and journals of varying distinction. It is, of course, possible that some of the people now busily engaged in this fashionable pursuit believe that they are doing so from pure and benevolent motives.

There is, however, evidence of a certain moral or political asymmetry in their behavior so far. It seems that they are concerned mainly with the intelligence services of the West. The list of names and addresses appearing in various publications in Paris, London and in the United States are, so it is claimed, those of members of the American Central Intelligence Agency.

These same people, you may notice, have not yet come up with a list of the names and addresses of agents of the Soviet KGB [secret police] or the Czechoslovak Intelligence Service working in London, Paris or Washington.

This is not because this information is not available. I could, if the editor of *The Times* [of London] felt able to devote the space to such a project, fill a large proportion of this page with a list which would be at least as accurate as those now being published of the Central Intelligence Agency.

I could, furthermore, embellish it with such fascinating

[6] Article entitled "World Nation-State Structure Makes Intelligence Essential," by Lord Chalfont (Alun Gwynne-Jones), British Minister for Disarmament 1964-1970, author of books on defense. Text from New York *Times*. p 13. F. 15, '76. Reproduced from *The Times* by permission. © 1976 by Times Newspapers Ltd.

extras as the names of KGB agents who have been expelled from . . . [Britain] and who are now plying their trade in Bangkok and other sensitive Southeast Asian capitals. I shall not do so because I regard the whole business as stupidly irresponsible; indeed it would be possible to describe it as puerile if it were not, in fact, sometimes tragically dangerous, as it turned out to be in the case of the American recently murdered in Athens.

The fact is that intelligence officers are well aware of the identity of their opposite numbers. Generally speaking, whatever may be suggested by the more sensational kind of novel and television film, they do not go about murdering each other. When names and addresses are made public, however, those identified are vulnerable to every crank or psychopath with the price of a revolver or a stick of gelignite.

It is, of course, arguable that espionage, in its conventional sense, is archaic and irrelevant, even in a world of nation-states.

Those countries who wish to discover the military, economic and political secrets of other countries are now able to do so through the agency of an astonishing range of electronic and other devices ranging from reconnaissance satellites taking high-definition photographs to remotely controlled listening-and-recording devices of almost unbelievable precision and refinement.

Yet the secret agent still exists, sometimes because he provides the only means of obtaining some specific type of information, and sometimes because he is, as an "agent of influence," able to affect the course of political decision-making in the country to which he is assigned.

All this, of course, will enrage those who believe that the world of the nation-state, with its paraphernalia of armaments, diplomacy and espionage, is old fashioned and immoral, and that we should be living together as a peaceful world community, irrespective of race, nationality, color or creed. As desirable as such a world may be, it is not the one in which we live; and until we achieve it, we had better learn to make the best of what we have.

What we have, among other things, is an international system in which every power of any size or consequence has a secret intelligence service. To the citizens of this country the most significant and important manifestation of this occurs in the persistent confrontation between the Communist world represented by the Soviet Union and its allies, and the non-Communist world represented by the United States of America and its allies.

In the pursuit of their respective interests these conflicting groups employ clandestine means, including espionage and, by extension, counterespionage; and even to the most neutral and uncommitted observer it must be obvious that however squalid and repellent the whole business may be, it is illogical to apply double standards to it.

If it is outrageous that the CIA should kill, blackmail and terrorize in the pursuit of its unappetizing trade, then it is equally outrageous that the KGB should do so; and even on this somewhat artificial basis the intrepid scribes of the underground press ought not to direct their attention exclusively at the intelligence services of the West.

It is, however, as I have suggested, an artificial argument, because very few people on either side *are* neutral. Most people believe in and are, in one degree or another, committed to the survival of their own system.

The political system under which we live in the West is riddled with imperfections. It does, however, embody a degree of individual liberty and a respect for freedom of choice and human dignity which many of us regard as the indispensable basis of a civilized existence.

The Communist system, as it has developed in the Soviet Union and in most of the countries of Eastern Europe, is oppressive, degrading and often shockingly cruel. Furthermore, there is evidence of an undiminished determination on the part of the Soviet Union to export that system to as much of the rest of the world as will accept it.

There are, according to the precepts and tactics of Marxism-Leninism, a number of possible ways in which this can be done, some of them peaceful, employing the instruments of trade, diplomacy and political persuasion.

The instrument of armed force is not ruled out, however, if other methods should prove ineffective and if war should offer a reasonable possibility of success. Now, this is where we all have to decide which side we are on.

If the Soviet Union and its allies in the Warsaw Pact decided to mount an armed attack on the Western alliance, most of us would recognize that the armed forces of NATO, including those of the United States, were engaged in our defense. We would rightly condemn unequivocally anyone who deliberately engaged in actions designed to undermine their effectiveness.

If that attitude makes sense—and I believe it does—then it should apply with equal force in a situation in which international communism is employing its alternative instruments of expansion, subversion and infiltration.

In this case, our defense is not a military one. It involves a whole complex of diplomatic and political activity, of which espionage and counterintelligence are an integral part. Yet we have seen, in recent months, a coordinated attack on the American Central Intelligence Agency which has materially affected the security of the United States and of the West as a whole.

We are, evidently, prepared to tolerate behavior in the press which, in time of more formal and conventional war, would be regarded as treasonable and therefore punishable. It is, surely, time we recognized clearly this latest example of the use of democratic instruments—in this case the freedom of the press—to undermine the very foundations of our democratic systems.

If the people now engaged in what they refer to as "spook-spotting" are really outraged by espionage and secret intelligence operations as a manifestation of human behavior, then let us reveal the names and addresses of Communist agents working in the West. They are, as I have already suggested, readily available.

If on the other hand the campaign continues to be directed exclusively at the intelligence organizations of the West, those who are engaged in it must not be surprised if they are themselves regarded as enemy agents. Someone, indeed, might one day start publishing *their* names and addresses—strictly, of course, in the public interest.

INTELLIGENCE, MORALITY, AND FOREIGN POLICY [7]

In the conduct of foreign affairs, as in personal matters, there are situations in which silence or secrecy demonstrates a form of morality. There are also times when secrecy alone is not enough: The defense of a free society or the maintenance of peace in the world may require the uncovering of complex information about the committed adversaries of freedom. If, in that process, abuses develop in the intelligence systems of a free nation, then appropriate methods must be devised for safely counteracting the morally illegitimate activities. We must unquestionably, however, maintain *intelligent* intelligence operations.

There are at least three fundamental questions whose answers have a direct bearing on the conduct and outcome of American foreign policy. The first is whether the normal

[7] Article by Sidney Hook, emeritus professor of philosophy at New York University, senior fellow at Hoover Institution on War, Revolution and Peace, Stanford University. *Freedom at Issue*. no 35:3-7. Mr.-Ap. '76. Reprinted by permission of Freedom House, 20 W. 40th St., New York 10018.

political process can cope effectively with the problems and perennial crises of foreign policy, or whether this is a domain in which ultimate decisions must be entrusted to a dedicated corps of trained specialists responsible to the executive power. The second is whether principles of morality can and should operate in guiding the conduct of foreign policy, and to what extent the national interest should be subordinated to such principles when their role is acknowledged. The third is what moral choices are open to a democratic nation like our own in a world in which it is threatened by aggressive totalitarian powers and ideologies.

From [French historian] de Tocqueville to [American author and editor] Walter Lippmann democracies have been faulted because of their inability to conduct intelligent foreign policies. The argument is quite familiar. Where domestic policies are concerned their fruits can be roughly but properly determined by consequences perceived not too long after they have been adopted. If unsatisfactory, they can be corrected or agitation against them developed. But the consequences of a foreign policy are rarely immediate. Critical judgment usually follows only after the experience of bitter fruits of disaster. On the other hand, where the urgencies of a crisis situation require immediate response the democratic process is too slow and unwieldy. It is therefore concluded that because of the delicacy, complexity and sometimes the necessary secrecy of foreign policy negotiations and actions, because the strategies to meet acts of foreign aggression must be initiated before their outcome confronts the nation and limits its choice of alternatives of response, there is great danger to the national interest—today even to national survival—in deferring to the vagaries of public opinion that tend to swing pendularly from one extreme to another. De Tocqueville's words are often cited to drive these points home:

Foreign politics demand scarcely any of those qualities which a democracy possesses; and they require, on the contrary, the perfect use of almost all those faculties in which it is deficient. . . . A democracy is unable to regulate the details of an important undertaking, to persevere in a design, and to work out its execution in the presence of serious obstacles. It cannot combine its measures with secrecy, and it will not await their consequences with patience.

De Tocqueville's indictment can be substantiated from the historical record. When memories of past wars are faint, public opinion can too easily be aroused in support of armed conflict. This was apparent in 1914. And once hostilities begin, the slogans of total victory or unconditional surrender become extremely popular. Proposals for a negotiated peace are denounced as treasonable. On the other hand, after a costly war popular opinion is apt to become fearful and defeatist and to resist policies which, had they been adopted in time, might have prevented the very outcome that was feared most. The popular opposition to the rearmament of Britain in the thirties is a case in point. Another is the failure to act vigorously—urged only by two public figures, Pilsudski [Polish general and statesman] and Trotsky [Russian Communist leader]—against Hitler's reentry into the Rhineland in defiance of the Treaty of Versailles. And although it is often ignored, the capitulation to Hitler at Munich was approved with wild popular enthusiasm as insuring peace in our time.

Other considerations make much of the instability and ignorance of popular opinion. Those who stress them tend to argue that the only alternative to the paralysis of the national will in foreign policy in a nation like our own is not to share the power but to entrust it to the Executive branch. In an address delivered in New York in 1963, Senator [J.W.] Fulbright [Democrat, Arkansas, 1945-1974, chairman of Foreign Relations Committee] voiced sentiments in this vein which contrast sharply with some of his later pronouncements:

> Public opinion must be educated and led if it is to bolster a wise and effective foreign policy. This is preeminently a task for presidential leadership because the presidential office is the only one under our constitutional system that constitutes a forum for moral and political leadership on a national scale. Accordingly I think that we must contemplate the further enhancement of presidential authority in foreign affairs.

Whose Business Is Foreign Policy?

Granted all this and more, there are overwhelming considerations that make it dubious to entrust the direction of foreign policy (always excluding specific emergency actions whose continuation must be subject to later congressional ratification) to the exclusive purview of the executive power. First, in a democratic community which assumes that those who are affected by basic decisions should have some voice in influencing them, foreign policy must be a matter of high public concern. Especially today in the era of nuclear technology, foreign policy may center on decisions that spell national freedom or enslavement, or the life and death of tens of millions. Foreign policy is everybody's business.

Second, where US foreign policy has been determined by the Executive independently of public opinion, the consequences have not been very happy for the preservation of freedom and the safeguarding of peace. Woodrow Wilson, elected in 1916 to keep the country out of World War I, a year later took the United States into war and in all likelihood prevented a negotiated peace. Even if the Central Powers had emerged from the conflict relatively stronger than the Allied Powers, Lenin and his faction would probably not have come to power in Russia. (Kerensky [Russian revolutionary leader, prime minister July-November 1917] has admitted that the continuation of the war was a decisive factor in their triumph.) Without Lenin, the socialist and labor movements of Italy and Germany would not have been disastrously split and we might have been spared Mussolini and Hitler, not to speak of Stalin and Mao. In any event, no matter who had won, in the absence of American intervention it would be hard to imagine a world worse than the Nazi and Gulag archipelagos.

Roosevelt during the Second World War regarded the Soviet Union as a genuine ally rather than as a cobelligerent, allaying deep popular distrust of the Kremlin's postwar intentions. Truman expressed Roosevelt's policy in the remark addressed to Senator [Burton K.] Wheeler's committee which waited on him, after his accession to the presidency, to caution against the extension of Soviet rule in Eastern Europe: "Gentlemen, it is not Soviet communism I fear but rather British imperialism"—and this on the eve of the grant of independence to India and the disintegration of the British Empire.

Third, in the long run the success of any foreign policy, even when initiated by the Executive in a crisis, as was the case in Korea (a needless war largely precipitated by the withdrawal of American troops and the declaration that Korea was outside the bounds of our national interest) depends upon the understanding and support of the people. The disaster in Vietnam to a large extent flowed from the absence of popular understanding of what justified our continued presence there after the initial error of involvement had been made.

There are good pragmatic grounds therefore for sharing with the citizenry the determination of foreign policy.

Morality in Public Affairs

This brings to the fore the second question—one that can be posed in the form of a further criticism of a democratic approach to foreign policy. It is often argued that popular influence on foreign policy is undesirable because it tends to be naive and moralistic. It assumes that what is good or bad, right or wrong, honorable or dishonorable, in private ordinary life is no less so in the life of nations at peace or at war. But many experts in foreign policy assure us that standards of morality in private and public life are profoundly different. Who does not recall the words of statesmen warning against a too simple identification of personal and public morality? Cavour, the Italian statesman [1810-1861], not the worst of the great unifiers, uttered a sentiment that all of them would have approved: "If we did for ourselves what we did for our country, what scoundrels we would be."

Our former Secretary of State Dean Acheson, in an address to those contemplating a career in foreign service, observed ". . . generally speaking, morality often imposes upon those who exercise the powers of government standards of conduct quite different from what might seem right to them as private citizens."

Although this is a plausible and widely held view, it seems to me to rest on a confusion between moral standards or basic moral values, which if valid, are invariant for all situations in which human beings must act and the specific situations in which the decision must be made. No moral principle by itself determines what action should be taken because, when we are in an agony of doubt about what we should do, more than one moral principle applies. This is as true in the area of personal relations as in public policy. Because we should tell the truth, it does not follow that we should tell the truth to someone intent upon killing or maiming or robbing others, if not telling the truth will tend to prevent such action. There are always other values involved. Even in less extreme situations we may rightly prefer to be kind rather than needlessly truthful if the truth speaking will result in great cruelty and no benefit to anyone else.

It is wrong to steal but we cannot morally condemn the man who steals to provide food for his starving family if no other means exist to alleviate their condition. Every situation of moral choice is one in which the choice is not between good and bad, right or wrong but between good and good, right and right, the good and the right. One good may be overridden by a greater good: one obligation by a more pressing one. Ordinary human life would be impossible if we did not recognize and act on these considerations. It is wrong to kill a human being but *if the only way* to prevent him from blowing up a plane or city was by killing him it would be right to do so. To be sure the weight of experience is behind the moral injunctions and ideals expressed in the testaments and commandments of the great religions and ethical systems of the past. But they cannot all be categorical in all situations because they sometimes conflict. Reflection is required in order to determine which is to be subordinate to which. The only moral absolute is, to use a phrase of [American educator] John Erskine's, the moral obligation to be intelligent in the choice we make of that course of conduct among possible alternatives whose consequences will strengthen the structure of the reflective values that define our philosophy of life.

This does not justify some current degenerate forms of existentialism according to which individuals are free to decide for themselves what is right or wrong without any appeal to moral principles or ideals but merely on the basis of what they desire. They seem to assume that because principles or ideals do not possess an absolutely categorical character that therefore they have no validity whatsoever. They thereby overlook the fact that when a legitimate exception is made to a moral rule, this does not destroy the validity and binding character of that rule within certain limits and conditions. They fail to recognize the overriding obligation of another rule that holds when the conditions are different. The better is the enemy of the good, and the bad is preferable to what is worse—when these are the only alternatives.

The situation is quite familiar in the area of civil and political rights. We all know that the right to know may conflict with the right to privacy, the freedom to publish may destroy a person's right to a fair trial, the freedom to speak (falsely to shout Fire! in a crowded theatre) with the right to life. Even the right to worship according to one's conscience may be abridged if it involves human sacrifice or polygamy. In this country it is the Supreme Court which determines the order of priority these freedoms have and under what conditions. In England, it is Parliament. None of these rights can be considered as absolute in the sense that they can never be overriden in any circumstance.

It is when we approach the field of foreign policy that the greatest confusion abounds. A foreign policy must further the interests and safety of the nation. But any nation worthy of the support of moral men and women must be committed to certain moral ideals—freedom, self-determination, peace and human welfare. But no more in this case than in the case of personal morality does that mean that we can deduce what our policy should be in specific foreign policy situations. If we espouse "the right to self-determination" as we should, that will not mean that in any and every circumstance of international affairs, we should support it, regardless of other moral values involved, any more than that we should always tell the truth about everything to everyone, or give alms in any and every circumstance. Self-determination is one value among others and we must evaluate a claim for it in a specific case in the light of its consequences on these other values. Not every province of every country that raises the cry warrants our support any

more than the demand for self-determination of the south-
ern states warranted moral support when they sought to
dissolve the Union. If a country or region of a country demands self-determination in order to impose slavery on
others or to unleash an aggressive war there is good reason
not to support it. No group that raises the banner of self-
determination really believes that the principle should be
universalized. Indian intellectuals under British rule were
eloquent about self-determination but they regarded the
slogan as treasonable when raised by the inhabitants of
Goa and Kashmir. The same was true for the Greek
Cypriots in relation to the Turkish enclaves after independence was won by Cyprus.

Morality and the National Interest

There are those who are impatient with considerations
about moral principles where national interest is involved.
They take as their guide Lord Palmerston's pronouncement:
"We have no eternal allies and we have no eternal enemies.
Our interests are eternal and perpetual, and those interests
it is our duty to follow." [Palmerston was Britain's prime
minister 1855-1858 and 1859-1865.] In the light of American
relations with Russia and China in the past sixty years one
can certainly agree with this but read a different implication
out of it. Why should the national interest exclude moral
ideals? Despite the ambiguities and complexities of the concept of national interest, it presupposes at the very least
national survival. Even on the plane of personal morality,
survival—except under extraordinary conditions—is integral
to the good life. In order to be blessed, says Spinoza [17th
century Dutch philosopher] one must at least be. The real
question is how narrowly the national interest is to be conceived. We are not talking about national survival under any
circumstances but of our survival as a free and open society.
To some moral and patriotic Frenchmen the acceptance of

Churchill's proposal to Vichy to accept union with Great Britain, even if this meant that France as a separate nation would exist no more, was preferable to the continued existence of France under Fascist rule.

Once the survival of our free society with all its imperfections and limitations is regarded as desirable, to what measures are we therewith committed in its defense? Certainly not to any measures regardless of their consequences to our security and the character of the society we seek to defend. The untenability of the doctrine that the end of national security justifies the use of any means to insure it is, first, that often the means employed are *not* the most intelligent means of securing that end; and, second, that the consequences of using some means may adversely and unacceptably affect the constellation of other ends—our institutionalized rights, freedoms and services—whose security we are defending. Nonetheless there are occasions when the ends and values whose presence defines a free and open society conflict, and we must choose between them. There are occasions when freedom of the press does severely prejudice a person's right to a fair trial. There are occasions when speech is used to incite a lynch mob to deprive a person of life or limb. At any definite time the conflict of freedoms is resolved or should be resolved by the action whose consequences are more likely than those of any other action to further the total structure of freedoms in the community. Normally the suspension of freedom of the press for a few days with respect to certain features of a case, with unlimited freedom to comment subsequently, is considered by reflective judgment to be less undesirable than the miscarriage of justice that may result if such freedom remains unabridged. Some of those who protest in the interests of a free press that there is an absolute right to know in such cases do not extend it to the right to know the sources that the press relies on in its investigatory reports.

The great danger, of course, in invoking the sanctions of national security to curb any of the normal traditional freedoms of the marketplace of ideas is that the national security may not be involved at all, that it may be used as a pretext for arbitrary and illegal personal or factional interest. Measures that under proper safeguards may sometimes be both morally and legally legitimate in times of clear and present danger to the national security of the nation may be abused and misemployed against fellow citizens with whom we differ about policies. This was illustrated in the Watergate episode in which opponents *within* the democratic process were treated as if they were *enemies* of the democratic process.

How Defend the Free Society?

This makes focal the third question: What moral choices are open to a democratic society faced by an armed and powerful enemy whose declared objective is the destruction of free institutions like our own? If our society with all its imperfections—and with its multiple mechanisms for improvement—is worth surviving, it is worth defending. How can it legitimately defend itself?

At this point it is necessary to distinguish between two types of totalitarian powers and ideologies. Although as democrats we are morally committed to condemning both, both are not of the same direct and pressing concern to a culture that seeks to preserve its freedom. The first type has very unpleasant consequences for citizens who live within its borders but such nations do not threaten the peace of the world—for example, Franco's Spain and Tito's Yugoslavia. We need no present defense against them. The other type is aggressive and expansionist. It seeks overtly and sometimes covertly to undermine the strength and security of free countries and their allies. Today that characterizes the policy of the Soviet Union and in lesser measure, Commu-

nist China. The nature of the struggle to defend and preserve the free world requires at the very least some measures
of secrecy. For example, any agreement on multilateral
limitation on nuclear weapons is not worth the paper it is
written on unless there exists some method of checking on
the performance of the principals. If the United States has
discovered a method of checking compliance by the Soviet
Union, making such knowledge public would invite the
Kremlin to devise methods of escaping detection of violations and encourage it to stockpile nuclear weapons to a
point where its predominance would make it relatively in-
vulnerable to any response the United States could make if
the Kremlin launched a nuclear Pearl Harbor. Secrecy on
these and related matters is an axiom of political morality
one is tempted to write, of political sanity.

Our secrecy is not enough. We require in the interests of
our defense—and of the peace of the world—intelligence information concerning the Kremlin's success in penetrating
our secrecy and its progress in devising methods by which it
can undermine our defense. What is true for military
measures, *mutatis mutandis,* is true for some political
measures, too.

What this entails is that "intelligence measures" be intelligent. The revelations concerning certain unsavory and
foolish CIA operations is not an argument for the abolition
of the agency but for its improvement. As well argue that
we can remedy defective vision by poking the eyes out of
our head, as that the best way of correcting the shortcom-
ings of past intelligence practices is to abolish its functions;
or, what is tantamount to the same thing, make the details
of its operations known to a large congressional committee
whose staffs are in a position to leak secrets to the press.
Great Britain and every other democratic nation in the
world has an Official Secrets Act or something equivalent.
While such an act has never been necessary in America, our

system does anticipate that officials and journalists alike will demonstrate a high sense of responsibility. Each must be aware of the inevitable and necessary tension between governmental secrecy and the need of the public to know: yet each must recognize, in the absence of an absolute demarcation of their respective territories, that *some* secrecy is essential to survival of freedom, and each has the duty to discover where the invisible line rests in each situation.

There have undoubtedly been abuses in CIA activities, particularly in the failure to abide by the restrictions on the field of its surveillance. But these could have been exposed and corrected without destroying the effectiveness of intelligence operations abroad. In other words there is an intelligent way of revealing the inadequacies of intelligence services and an unintelligent way which profits no one but the KGB and other enemies of the relatively free nations of the world.

There seems to be a willful blindness among some commentators about the necessary role of intelligence services in the defense of a free and open society in an era in which the sudden death of a culture is possible. The blindness is sometimes reinforced by a smug moral posturing which confuses principles with tactical measures. The same considerations—the health and integrity of the democratic process —that condemn the giving of a bribe to a domestic official *may* justify the offer of a bribe to an official of a foreign country for information—not procurable in time by any other way—that may be crucial to the national safety.

Those who on *a priori* grounds condemn an action without regard for its consequences in preserving the structure of democratic freedoms are guilty at the very least of blatant hypocrisy. This does not give *carte blanche* to any fool to undertake any project because it seems to him advantageous at the moment. Here as elsewhere there is no substitute for intelligence—for intelligence ultimately responsible to the authorized representatives, legislative or judicial, of the democratic community. It is sometimes necessary to burn a house, or to permit it to burn, in order to save a village. This does not bestow a license for arson. We must recognize the evil we do even when it is the lesser evil. But if it is truly the lesser evil than those who condemn it or would have us do nothing at all are morally responsible for the greater evil that may ensue.

III. AFTER THE INVESTIGATION: OVERSIGHT AND REFORM

EDITOR'S INTRODUCTION

This final section deals with the questions which continue to exist, answers to which will determine the future course of intelligence in the United States.

"Out of sight, out of mind," goes an old saying, and it may never have been truer than in the case of public interest in the inquiry into the nation's intelligence operations. The first article in this section is an excerpt from the final report of the Senate Select Committee on Intelligence Activities, which became public at the end of April 1976. By early June it became virtually impossible to find in print, or other media, public discussion of the role of intelligence in American society—a subject that had been for many months top priority news. Leslie Gelb's article from the New York *Times* offers explanations of why public outrage ended in public indifference. Whatever the reasons, most of the basic questions, philosophical and operational, raised about American intelligence activity remained only half explored. The matter was kept alive, however, as is evidenced by the Columbia Law Symposium report that follows—a discussion by four experts in the field of intelligence on the theme "Can Our Freedom Survive Defense by the CIA and the FBI?"

Perhaps the intelligence community has been shaken sufficiently by the exposure of its own misdeeds that it will better police its own activities now and in the future. The next three articles, two of them by former CIA directors, deal with the investigations and the revelations and with the effects of these, both damaging and salutary, on the intelligence establishment, suggesting possible ways of ensuring that CIA operations in the future will be up to acceptable moral and legal standards.

Considerable argument has been put forth to support the thesis that further public discussion of American intelligence may be destructive, undermining its valid role in the national security structure, and that such discussion might even inhibit serious efforts underway to correct previous errors in organization and action. Perhaps this is true. Unfortunately there is no way for the public to judge, since the matter of intelligence operations has returned to its original (and historical) position—*out of sight*.

It seems obvious that reform must be accomplished. The final article in this section, by Harry Rositzke, a former CIA officer and specialist on foreign intelligence, offers the most detailed and informed suggestions yet made on the proper sphere of activity for American intelligence. Throughout the article, Rositzke uses the term AIS (American Intelligence Service) to indicate the whole range of secret action engaged in by the United States through existing agencies such as the CIA, DIA, and FBI. His proposed restructuring of the AIS would, essentially, relieve the CIA of its covert espionage role while preserving its principal intelligence functions. Responsibility for paramilitary operations would be shifted to the Department of Defense. Rositzke recognizes the need for the continuation of covert foreign espionage but places the function outside of the existing intelligence structure. This separation of functions, he suggests, would achieve greater security and efficiency—and with greater accountability.

SENATE SELECT COMMITTEE REPORT: SUMMARY OF FINDINGS AND RECOMMENDATIONS [1]

General Findings

The committee finds that United States foreign and military intelligence agencies have made important contributions to the nation's security, and generally have performed their missions with dedication and distinction. The committee further finds that the individual men and women serving America in difficult and dangerous intelligence assignments deserve the respect and gratitude of the nation.

The committee finds that there is a continuing need for an effective system of foreign and military intelligence. United States interests and responsibilities in the world will be challenged, for the foreseeable future, by strong and potentially hostile powers. This requires the maintenance of an effective American intelligence system. The committee has found that the Soviet KGB and other hostile intelligence services maintain extensive foreign intelligence operations, for both intelligence collection and covert operational purposes. These activities pose a threat to the intelligence activities and interests of the United States and its allies.

The committee finds that Congress has failed to provide the necessary statutory guidelines to insure that intelligence agencies carry out their missions in accord with constitutional processes. Mechanisms for and the practice of congressional oversight have not been adequate. Further, Congress has not devised appropriate means to effectively use the valuable information developed by the intelligence

[1] Excerpts from *Report on Foreign and Military Intelligence Activities of the United States*, report of the Senate Select Committee to Study Governmental Operations With Respect to Intelligence Activities. Text from New York *Times*. p. 21. Ap. 27, '76.

agencies. Intelligence information and analysis that exist within the Executive branch clearly would contribute to sound judgments and more effective legislation in the areas of foreign policy and national security.

The committee finds that covert action operations have not been an exceptional instrument used only in rare instances when the vital interests of the United States have been at stake. On the contrary, Presidents and Administrations have made excessive, and at times self-defeating, use of covert action. In addition, covert action has become a routine program with a bureaucratic momentum of its own. The long-term impact, at home and abroad, of repeated disclosure of US covert action never appears to have been assessed. The cumulative effect of covert actions has been increasingly costly to America's interests and reputation. The committee believes that covert action must be employed only in the most extraordinary circumstances.

Although there is a question concerning the extent to which the Constitution requires publication of intelligence expenditures information, the committee finds that the Constitution at least requires public disclosure and public authorization of an annual aggregate figure for US national intelligence activities. Congress' failure as a whole to monitor the intelligence agencies' expenditures has been a major element in the ineffective legislative oversight of the intelligence community. The permanent intelligence oversight committee (s) of Congress should give further consideration to the question of the extent to which further public disclosure of intelligence budget information is prudent and constitutionally necessary.

At the same time, the committee finds that the operation of an extensive and necessarily secret intelligence system places severe strains on the nation's constitutional government. The committee is convinced, however, that the competing demands of secrecy and the requirements of the democratic process—our Constitution and our laws—can be reconciled. The need to protect secrets must be balanced with the assurance that secrecy is not used as a means to hide the abuse of power or the failures and mistakes of policy. Means must and can be provided for lawful disclosure of unneeded or unlawful secrets.

The committee finds that intelligence activities should not be regarded as ends in themselves. Rather, the nation's intelligence functions should be organized and directed to assure that they serve the needs of those in the executive and legislative branches who have responsibility for formulating or carrying out foreign and national security policy.

The committee finds that Congress has failed to provide the necessary statutory guidelines to insure that intelligence agencies carry out their necessary missions in accord with constitutional process.

In order to provide firm direction for the intelligence agencies, the committee finds that new statutory charters for these agencies must be written which take account of the experience of the past three and a half decades. Further, the committee finds that the relationship among the various intelligence agencies and between them and the director of Central Intelligence should be restructured in order to achieve better accountability, coordination and more efficient use of resources.

These tasks are urgent. They should be undertaken by the Congress in consultation with the Executive branch in the coming year. The recent proposals and executive actions by the President are most welcome. [See "Laws, Men, and the CIA," by Anthony Lewis, in Section II, above.] However, further action by Congress is necessary.

Recommendations

1. The National Security Act should be recast by omnibus legislation which would set forth the basic purposes of

national intelligence activities, and define the relationship between the Congress and the intelligence agencies of the Executive branch. This revision should be given the highest priority by the intelligence oversight committee of Congress, acting in consultation with the Executive branch.

2. The new legislation should define the charter of the organization and entities in the US intelligence community. It should establish charters for the National Security Council, the director of Central Intelligence, the Central Intelligence Agency, the national intelligence components of the Department of Defense, including the National Security Agency and the Defense Intelligence Agency, and all other elements of the intelligence community, including joint organizations of two or more agencies.

3. This legislation should set forth the general structure and procedures of the intelligence community and the roles and responsibilities of the agencies which comprise it.

4. The legislation should contain specific and clearly defined prohibitions or limitations on various activities carried out by the respective components of the intelligence community.

OUTRAGE TURNS TO INDIFFERENCE [2]

The congressional and presidential investigations into domestic spying and political assassination plots by the intelligence community began . . . [in February 1975] amid public outrage but are now ending amid public indifference and congressional uncertainty over whether there will eventually be adequate reforms.

"It all lasted too long, and the media, the Congress and the people lost interest," commented Representative Otis

[2] Article entitled "Spy Inquiries, Begun in Outrage, End in Indifference," by Leslie H. Gelb, journalist, staff correspondent for New York *Times*. New York *Times.* p 20. My. 12, '76. © 1976 by The New York Times Publishing Company. Reprinted by permission.

G. Pike [Democrat, New York], who headed the House Select Committee on Intelligence. The House voted against publishing his committee's report and ignored its proposals for a basic structural overhaul of the intelligence community.

Administration officials take the position that President Ford has already done enough to reinforce and streamline policy control of intelligence activities and catch abuses, but mostly through changes that are being kept secret, even from Congress.

Senator Frank Church [Democrat, Idaho], chairman of the Senate Select Committee [to Study Governmental Operations With Respect to Intelligence Activities], has argued that it is not enough for the President to put the Administration's own house in order. The Church committee has pushed for a new congressional oversight committee on intelligence, to consolidate and strengthen the current system, which is fragmented among several committees.

A Case Study

What began with sensational publicity accompanying disclosures of the intelligence inquiries is ending now in compromises. Why this happened and how it happened is a case study in the subtle ways in which the politics of . . . [Washington, D.C.] work.

Perhaps most important, the political climate has changed since the start of the investigations. Congress, once on the offensive, was thrown back somewhat on the defensive by disputes over disclosures of classified information given to congressional committees and over responsibility for the assassination in Greece of the chief of the Central Intelligence Agency operations there.

Then, as the details of covert operations, illegal wiretappings and mail openings became old news, public interest waned, and congressional committees and Executive agencies turned inward, settling their disputes along the usual lines of committee turf, bureaucratic tactics and access to information.

Equally fundamental, the personalities and strategies of the two congressional investigating committees diverged sharply, and thus Congress was unable to face the Administration with a solid front.

Mr. Pike tried to operate in the open and to confront the White House, and he lost support in the House. Mr. Church and his Senate committee made compromises, doing some things in the open and other things in private, and generally tried to get along with the Administration.

Support Is Sought

Now, he must shepherd support among—and sometimes against—the Senate leaders whose committees have long handled intelligence matters and who are reluctant to surrender these prerogatives to the new oversight committee he proposes.

Throughout, the congressional investigators have been hobbled by the difficulties of obtaining information on the inner workings of the intelligence community.

Some officials, noting the reluctance of the Administration to share information—and through it, power—with Congress, recalled that former Secretary of Defense James R. Schlesinger once told a White House meeting that sensitive information should not be given to the Pike committee because the committee contained unfriendly foreign operatives.

According to these sources, William E. Colby, then the director of Central Intelligence, ironically commented that this was a good idea, and he was sure that Mr. Schlesinger had evidence to support his allegation and should turn it over to House Speaker Carl Albert [Democrat, Oklahoma, retired 1976]. No more was said.

Even within the Executive branch, rivalries and sensitivities affected the flow of information. Vice President Rockefeller reportedly lectured Mr. Colby once for having given too much information to the commission set up within the Executive branch to investigate CIA activities. Mr. Rockefeller headed that commission himself.

More common apparently, was the frustration of the Executive branch investigators at the refusal of intelligence agencies to disclose enough about their past methods of operation. "There were times when we wished we had subpoena power here in the White House," one official said.

Another said that ultimately the Executive branch investigation succeeded, because the White House was able to play off the intelligence agencies against one another. The White House, he said, "was able to pry information out of the agencies, because each agency didn't know what the White House was getting from the others, and they were afraid of getting caught in a lie."

Confirmation that this tactic was effective came from a CIA official. "The biggest fear here," he said, "was the rest of the Executive branch more than Congress." Officials from other agencies made the same points. Each was concerned about opening up its secret sources and methods to the others.

Providing sensitive information to congressional committees was a separate problem. Early meetings of an interagency committee headed by John O. Marsh Jr., the President's counselor, were punctuated by a lot of speechmaking on the need for being rough with the committees. Attorney General Edward H. Levi would often interrupt to say something like: "This is a fine speech for Broadway, but how will it sound when they throw you in a cell for violating the law?"

The general view among officials in the Administration and on Capitol Hill who have been involved with the various investigations is that the main obstacles to turning over information came from those concerned with policy at the State and Defense departments, from the National Security Council staff and from the heads of operational staff.

Generally on the other side were the White House staff, which believed that President Ford had nothing to hide, and the leaders of the CIA, who believed that their agency could be saved only by being candid.

The President decided early to be more forthcoming with the Church committee than with the Pike committee. This was a reflection of the very different ways in which the committees sought to get information.

Mr. Pike was made chairman of the House committee largely because of the majority's conviction that Representative Lucien Nedzi, the chairman of the House Armed Services Committee, had not been tough enough in his oversight. Mr. Pike hired a young staff with few Washington ties, and together they confronted the Administration at each step. Committee unity fell apart when Mr. Pike recommended citing Mr. Kissinger for contempt when he did not turn over certain policy papers.

Mr. Church, on the other hand, gave high priority to holding his committee together. He built a staff of experienced congressional aides, and their approach was to cajole and cooperate with the Administration.

Diversion and Delay

For the Church committee, getting all the assassination material set an important precedent for obtaining additional documents. But the very volume of the assassination material forced diversion and delay. Months were spent preparing that report before the bulk of the committee got down to its assigned business.

But in the long run, the Pike committee's confrontation tactics may have hurt, leaving the Senate committee's campaign for stronger congressional oversight of intelligence activities without a corresponding effort in the House. The tactics also changed the focus of debate in Washington from how much congressional oversight is necessary to whether Congress can keep a secret.

Mr. Pike sees some advantage to his tough stance, however. "I think Church paid a price for cooperation," the Representative says. "Less information was made public."

In this respect, there was a dovetailing of strategies between the White House and the Church committee. "The President's attitude was that there was no reason to keep information respecting mistakes and abuses from Congress," one White House official explained, "but at the same time, the President felt he had the responsibility that it not be made public if it would damage the country."

Most Administration officials maintained that the President had no grand strategy for dealing with Congress, except to avoid any appearance of a cover-up and to conclude the investigations as quickly as possible. "The longer it went on, the more rocks would be turned over, the more worms would be found," one key participant said.

Delay was inherent in the practical steps taken by the Administration to insure its concepts of secrecy. One who took part in the process of negotiation said:

"If the committee asked for information, we'd brief them. If they demanded the documents, we'd give them a sanitized version. If this wasn't enough, we'd give them the rest on the condition they would not publish without consent."

Others in the Administration sought delay, one official said, "much the same way a lawyer plays for time, hoping something will come up to save his client." Things did come up.

"Pike, Welch and Schorr, those were the three names that caused us to pull back, not because our constituents said you're going too far, but because those names came to have important symbolic importance in the currency of Washington," said a Senator who did not want to be identified.

Richard S. Welch was the head of the CIA office in Greece. He was murdered shortly after a magazine identified him. Daniel Schorr was a reporter for CBS who obtained and arranged for publication of the still-classified Pike committee report [Schorr, citing his rights under the First Amendment refused the House Ethics Committee's demand to know the source of his information. The panel voted not to cite him for contempt. He has since resigned from CBS and will write and teach.—Ed.]

Senator Walter F. Mondale, Democrat of Minnesota [elected Vice President in 1976], who was a member of the Church committee, said: "There was a sense of anarchy over in the House. Then came the Welch murder and what I believe to be the careful orchestration of the Welch funeral to tie the murder to the congressional investigations."

Administration officials denied any orchestration, maintaining that all of the funeral arrangements were made by the Welch family.

"The Schorr matter," Mr. Mondale said, "further undermined confidence in Congress to deal with secret matters."

As the public became "numb with bad news," in Mr. Mondale's phrase, some members of the Pike committee apparently sought to revive public attention through unauthorized disclosures of information. Meanwhile, the Church committee continued to keep those secrets to show that Congress can do so and that congressional oversight can work.

From the start, the Church committee's goal, according to committee members, was to generate support for standing congressional oversight committees, with full legislative and budgetary authority and new laws governing intelligence activities.

To some members of the Pike committee, his goals, in some respects, went much deeper—to a basic restructuring of the intelligence community—and much beyond what the House and the Administration seemed prepared to support.

The Pike committee wanted to know how much intelligence costs the taxpayer and whether the results were worth the costs and the risks. The committee's report, which has been criticized by many people, came to the conclusion that the taxpayer was not getting his money's worth. The national intelligence budget is estimated at $4.5 billion.

The Senate is now about to consider the Church committee's plan for a standing oversight committee that would supersede the three existing committees—Armed Services, Appropriations and Foreign Relations—with authority over intelligence agencies. [A permanent Select Committee On Intelligence was established in May 1976 with exclusive oversight authority.—Ed.]

The battle lines are drawn along these lines: On the one side are those who back the existing oversight committees and some who also feel that Congress ought not to get deeply involved in the President's business of running intelligence operations. On the other side are those who feel that the existing committees did not do the job.

A White House official who supports the President's proposal for a joint House-Senate oversight committee argued that the legislative and budgetary powers of the proposed new Senate committee go too far. "It makes the committee a participant in decisions, and how can it be both participant and judge?" he asked. "Who will then do the overseeing?"

The Church committee's report makes clear that it intended the proposed committee to be a participant and is less concerned about oversight as such. It is the power to decide that it wants to share with the President.

CAN OUR FREEDOMS SURVIVE DEFENSE
BY THE CIA AND FBI? [3]

"If publicity has become a necessary part of the cure, the disease must be pretty deep and serious," said Telford Taylor, Columbia's Nash Professor of Law.

"It is deep," commented Columbia Professor of Government Roger Hilsman, who was an assistant secretary of state during the Kennedy Administration, "and the cost to us has been enormous. Absolutely enormous. Not in money terms but in wasting one of the great assets we once had: the respect for our integrity and goals and methods."

"We have adopted the worst tactics of the Russians," agreed Frederick A. O. Schwarz Jr., who is the chief counsel for the Senate Select Committee to Study Governmental Operations With Respect to Intelligence Activities. "Our government, in the belief that it was defending freedom, used the tactics of totalitarianism: unfair tactics, vicious tactics, tactics that are wholly outside the best traditions of the United States.

"The excuse for such operations has been that our national security required these acts," said Paul C. Warnke, . . . who was Assistant Secretary of Defense for International Affairs under President [Lyndon B.] Johnson. "I would suggest that this is a flimsy excuse. It suggests a degree of danger to our national security that does not exist."

The CIA and the FBI: Is the uproar over their tactics justified? How has the scandal affected the United States? What should we do to prevent future scandals?

These were some of the issues considered by the men quoted above as they participated in a panel discussion held . . . [April 3, 1976] as part of Columbia Law Symposium, an

[3] Columbia Law Symposium report. *Columbia Today.* v 2, no 1:6-9. Je. '76. Published by The Trustees of Columbia University. Reprinted by permission.

annual event sponsored by the Columbia Law School Alumni Association. Professor Taylor, who moderated the discussion, introduced the other speakers, noting "their broad range of experience in the intelligence world."

Hilsman Offers Some Praise

"This is a world of sovereign nation states," Professor Hilsman pointed out. "We don't have a world government. Until we do, each nation must look to itself for its own security, and intelligence is part of that.

"And as intelligence agencies go, the CIA isn't a bad one. It has centralized our foreign intelligence gathering. It has done some simply marvelous jobs in technical fields— satellite photography and the U-2, for example.

"I remember Chester Bowles [government official, statesman, and noted author of books on foreign affairs] once saying: 'Thank God for the U-2. It showed us the Russians weren't as strong as we had suspected they might be.' If it hadn't been for the U-2, our defense budget in the cold war would have probably been twice what it actually was.

"But the CIA's most important contribution has been the perfectly legitimate, perfectly overt, analysis of thousands and thousands of periodical publications. This has been very well done.

"All the armed services start their planning with the National Intelligence Estimates, prepared under CIA chairmanship. Consider what the last twenty years would have been like if, in addition to the interservice rivalry we have had, each of the services would have started with its own intelligence estimates. Consider what it would have been like if Air Force planning had been based on intelligence documents dictated by Curtis LeMay!" [Major General Curtis LeMay was chief of staff USAF 1961-1965 and headed the Strategic Air Command for years.]

Warnke Agrees

"Good intelligence serves a number of very effective purposes. Certainly the national intelligence estimates have prevented gross miscalculations on the part of our defense planners.

"And if we did not have this tremendous intelligence capability, we would not have faith in the enforceability of disarmament agreements.

"Even intelligence on the part of the other side can be basically good for us. During the Six Day War in 1967, the Soviets were collecting data that enabled them to recognize the falsity of King Hussein's reports that the United States was participating in the air attack."

A Case for Covert Action?

"As long as it is a world of sovereign nations, there is a theoretical case for covert political action," said Professor Hilsman.

"For example, if you believe that World War II could have been avoided by the assassination of Hitler, then you have to admit that assassination is theoretically acceptable. I do not happen to believe that the removal of one man would do it.

"If you believe that it would have been possible to re-move the Nazi party in the mid-30s by encouraging a coup by the German General Staff, then covert political action must also be theoretically acceptable. I have grave doubts that even that would have been possible, though I concede the theoretical point.

"My own knowledge of covert political action is that it is of marginal value—that it has never worked except when the event probably would have happened anyway.

"For example, Allen Dulles used to take great credit for the removal of Mossadegh [premier of Iran 1951-1953] and the establishment of the Shah of Iran. My guess is that the change would have occurred even if the CIA had never existed.

"The covert actions in Chile were also marginal . . . and petty. What did the CIA do? They subsidized a newspaper. Does anyone really believe that one little newspaper caused the events in Chile? I don't. They subsidized the truckers' strike. Did that make the difference between a strike and no strike? I don't believe so. Everything I know about covert political action comes to that. The CIA takes credit for something that, by and large, I think would have happened anyway, without CIA intervention."

Undeserved Blame

Mr. Warnke pointed out that "covert activities have sometimes led to our being blamed for things we have not done."

"For example," he elaborated, "some Soviet officials now try to defend the 1968 Soviet invasion of Czechoslovakia on the grounds that they were entitled to counter American subversion there—the same sort of subversion that we later carried out in Chile. It is an excuse that in my opinion is without basis.

"But in the court of world opinion, we are in a sort of pot and kettle situation. Covert activities have weakened our ability to influence world affairs, and have seriously eroded the credibility and good will that the United States has been able to assemble over the years."

And in the United States

"The main threat to liberty in this country has been the FBI," said Mr. Schwarz. "For thirty or forty years, the FBI succeeded in convincing the American public that it was pure . . . that it was doing the right thing.

"And in the area of pursuing criminals, the Bureau has done, generally speaking, a good job. It is when it has crossed the line from surveillance of criminals to surveillance of dissenters—and to its subsequent actions against dissenters—that it has gone beyond what this country can tolerate under its Constitution.

"The Bureau has spent far too much money on dissent as opposed to its appropriate activities against crime. Even today, after certain cutbacks, it spends more than twice as much money on informers in the political community as it spends on informers in organized crime. This is a misallocation of resources. And under the Constitution it shouldn't be doing this at all.

"In the early 1970s, the Bureau covered all black student groups in colleges across the United States. Every single person who belonged to such a group was under surveillance and had a file created on him or her, regardless of whether or not that person—or that group—had participated in violent activities.

"The main violations of America's standards have occurred as part of the FBI's action programs, where they seek, as they put it, to 'neutralize, discredit, and disrupt' political groups.

"The targets of such activities have ranged from the famous, such as Martin Luther King, to the obscure. The King case is well known. Equally sad for our country have been the many, many people who were ordinary protestors —or who just associated with dissenters.

"One case that particularly sticks in my mind involved a thirty-year-old woman in Illinois whose husband was active in the civil rights movement. The Bureau decided to write a fake letter to her, complaining about the husband's sexual relations with people in the movement. Totally false. And then you see in the files of a federal government agency the notation: 'We have had the great effect of breaking up the people's marriage.' "

Sharing the Blame

The panelists indicated that responsibility for the illegalities committed by their agents does not rest solely with the CIA and FBI.

"The principal culprits have been the policymakers," said Professor Hilsman. "I want to hedge this by saying that if you give a very able group of people a lot of money, a secrecy label, and a very narrow responsibility, they are going to come up with ideas. And they are going to advocate and press their projects.

"Kennedy, for example, found himself under enormous pressure from Dulles and others to proceed with the Cuban invasion. That does not excuse him. He *could* have avoided it.

"So I am not saying that the CIA doesn't press Presidents. Generally speaking, however, it is the other way around. It has been the policymakers who have demanded that the Agency do something that it was either reluctant to do or not very enthusiastic about doing—or maybe enthusiastic about doing but not legally allowed to do. The people responsible for the Chile business were Richard Nixon and Henry Kissinger. It wasn't the Agency. Richard Nixon said, 'Do something about this situation.' And they did."

Mr. Schwarz mentioned that Congress also "played a very negative role" in the intelligence picture.

"Congress knew what the FBI was doing to Martin Luther King—and did nothing about it," Mr. Schwarz declared. "Congress also passed the Smith Act, which has led to the Bureau's justification of most surveillance activities." [The Smith Act was passed in 1940. It deals with penalties for advocating, teaching or advising the breaking of any law by force and/or advocating, teaching, advising, or conspiring to overthrow or oppose the US Government by force.—Ed.]

Congressional Oversight

One remedy considered by the panelists is the creation of a congressional oversight committee to monitor the activities of US intelligence agencies. (The Senate Select Committee on Intelligence Activities recommended the creation of such a committee in its report issued in late April [1976].)

"We need to return to the system of checks and balances planned by the Founding Fathers," said Mr. Schwarz. "When people can operate in secrecy, when they are subjected to the kinds of pressures that agents have been subjected to, and when they believe action is required, they will tend to operate against liberty; it's too easy. It's too hard to remember the restraints that are placed on power.

"We let the idea of secrecy, and the increasing power of the Executive, insulate from Congress and the American public—and the courts—the nature of the programs conducted in their name."

Professor Hilsman was skeptical: "Congressional committees, like regulatory agencies, get captured by the people they are supposed to oversee. I'm afraid that such a committee would become a powerful advocate and defender—and protector—of the agency."

Mr. Warnke also felt that "congressional oversight committees would not be a really effective answer."

"I'm also very skeptical of suggestions such as advanced clearance of proposed covert action by a congressional committee," he continued. "To the extent that a congressional committee shares the responsibility, it tends to take on the face of the regulated agency.

"Also, past experience with preclearance has not really been a happy one. Preclearance of covert activities smacks too much to me of a Tonkin Gulf resolution, in which the Executive comes to the Congress, secures a blank check, and then cashes it for a far greater amount than the Congress contemplated at the time the Executive presented it."

[After the Tonkin Gulf incident early in August of 1964 when North Vietnamese torpedo boats attacked US destroyers in the Gulf reporting intelligence information to South Vietnam, President Lyndon B. Johnson asked Congress for powers "to take all necessary measures to repel any armed attack against the forces of the United States and to prevent further aggression." Congress passed the resolution August 7.—Ed.]

Banning Covert Activities

Some people who have testified before congressional groups investigating CIA and FBI misdeeds have advocated that covert activities be banned entirely. Others maintain that such activities are justified in certain cases. [Former government official] McGeorge Bundy, for example, has suggested that covert activities would be acceptable to counter international terrorism or nuclear threats.

"I think I would preserve some sort of a covert action capability," said Mr. Warnke, "but I would do it on an ad hoc basis. I think there should be a presumption against it —a strong presumption. Only the most compelling of considerations ought to lead to the permission of covert activities.

"But there is no justification, under any circumstances, for covert *policy* or covert programs. Even if there is some justification for everyone not knowing how the government is trying to do something, everyone should know what his government is trying to do. Policies ought to be overt.

"This was demonstrated in connection with the Angolan debate [early in 1976], where at one point it was contemplated that we provide overt aid. And Secretary of State Kissinger, in a press conference, said no, we couldn't give overt aid because that would bring about a number of political and diplomatic problems.

"If we can't justify a program as part of an overt policy, there is no justification for doing it covertly."

Professor Hilsman suggested "legislation that flatly says 'no covert actions of any kind can be taken by the FBI and CIA.'

"I would also contemplate a law limiting the term of the director of the FBI, so the person couldn't build up power—as J. Edgar Hoover did."

Warnke Considers Ford's Proposals

In February of . . . [1976, President] Gerald Ford announced new guidelines for US intelligence agencies. His Executive order bans the use of assassination and sets some limits—considered ambiguous by critics of the plan—on the surveillance of US citizens. A three-man Committee on Foreign Intelligence, headed by the CIA director, will supervise, under the direction of the National Security Council.

President Ford's plan also establishes an Operations Advisory Group, composed of top Administration officials, that will review and vote on all proposed covert operations.

Mr. Warnke is "not at all sanguine about the effectiveness of the Executive order. First of all, a problem develops when you try to legislate against just certain things. The things that are not legislated against acquire a degree of sanction that perhaps they did not have before.

"This is the problem that exists as a result of the War Powers Resolution passed in late 1973. That legislation gave the President, for the first time, the explicit ability to conduct a war for a limited period of time, subject to congressional veto. Prior to passage of the resolution, I think a good argument could have been made that the President had no such power at all. So, while purporting to restrict Executive power, it in fact expanded the Executive's action capability.

"I think there should continue to be an Executive interdepartmental committee to review intelligence agency proposals and make recommendations to the President. This sort of committee can work—but not if the National Security Adviser is also the Secretary of State.

"I also think there should be an overall intelligence czar —one who would not have direct operational responsibilities in any one of the agencies. Theoretically, that has been the role of the director of Central Intelligence, but because he has an individual agency affiliation, he has sometimes been in the position of a competitor rather than an overseer."

Legislating Against Leaks

Mr. Warnke also had some comments about the threat to intelligence operations of leaks:

"I don't think the disclosures are seriously interfering with our intelligence gathering. Even the disclosures of names of agents abroad, though obviously reprehensible and of extreme danger to the individuals involved, does not really interfere with the core of our intelligence-gathering apparatus.

"It doesn't seem to me that the kind of legislation that has been proposed—to make it unlawful to leak information that you lawfully have in your possession—is ever going to be effective.

"In many instances, leaks are officially inspired. I remember one leak that greatly troubled President Johnson. He even went so far as to have the FBI investigate my own little shop. And eventually, it was proven that President Johnson had leaked the information while talking to a New York *Times* reporter.

"Some recent leaks of material gathered by congressional investigators may have been done to show the unreliability of Congress.

"Leaks are often designed to effect a particular purpose. Back in 1968, someone—subsequent investigation indicated that four separate sources were involved—leaked the fact that General Westmoreland had requested an additional 206,000 troops be sent to Vietnam. There were those who felt that the President would not be able to turn down the request once it was made public. Others obviously leaked it because they hoped public furor would prevent the request from being granted."

Law Is the Key

"The purpose of all the remedies," summarized Mr. Schwarz, "is not simply to protect American liberties at home but to restore the good name of the United States, so that once more it can be the last and best hope of mankind —which it basically still can be, but not if it operates in the way it has far too often in the past.

"Law is the key. We have departed from the law in the intelligence community, which has often justified its actions on the grounds of 'the greater good,' 'the higher good,' and 'national security.'"

Mr. Warnke believes that national security is "a flimsy excuse," suggesting a degree of danger that does not exist.

"There aren't very many threats to our security," he said. "The basic threat is the threat of Soviet military power. We aren't really in trouble as far as domestic insurrection is concerned. The Communist party in the United States represents as trivial a menace as the mind of man could devise. And I don't believe we are seriously threatened by changes overseas . . . by alterations in foreign governments.

"To avoid future abuses, we must get away from the idea that we are a beseiged outpost of freedom in a hostile world. We have friendly neighbors on both sides, and an ocean to the east and an ocean to the west.

"This doesn't mean that we can afford to become Fortress America or to be isolationists. It doesn't mean that we should forfeit our role in the world.

"But we should recognize that that role can be played usefully only through the exercise of our traditional American tolerance and by observing the civil liberties of both the United States and the rest of the world."

AFTER INVESTIGATING U.S. INTELLIGENCE [4]

A year of unprecedented investigation of United States intelligence has ended. It has not been the first investigation. Others followed Pearl Harbor, the Bay of Pigs and the exposure of Central Intelligence Agency assistance to foundations and voluntary associations. But those were conducted, as other nations do, by special boards of inquiry that made their investigations and took testimony in secret.

. . . [The 1976] investigations looked into the secret recesses. But they also brought the klieg lights of television to them as they probed. They did not result only in a final set of conclusions and recommendations.

Were they necessary? Were they effective? Were they damaging? Did something new emerge? The final assessment cannot yet be made, but I believe they have provided the foundation for a new meaning for the much-abused initials CIA—constitutional intelligence for America.

Necessary? After Vietnam, Watergate and sensational allegations that a rogue elephant was loose threatening our citizens and our good name—certainly. The public would no longer "shut your eyes" (as one member of Congress once suggested) to intelligence. And it would not be satisfied with a covering of "national security." Some public review and exposure was indeed necessary.

Effective? Yes. The investigation was facilitated by intelligence's own looks at itself. In 1973 it looked back for

[4] Article by William E. Colby, former CIA director; in Office of Strategic Services during World War II. New York *Times.* p 31. F. 26, '76. © 1976 by The New York Times Publishing Company. Reprinted by permission.

any "questionable activities" in its past, and directed that they be corrected for the future. On several occasions it criticized its own performance to find ways to improve itself. These self-examinations were made available to the investigating committees, which then checked them independently, and with sworn testimony, to find that indeed they were comprehensive.

Damaging? Yes, to a degree. The sensational atmosphere frightened many foreign friends of American intelligence. It caused a number of sources to withhold their cooperation. Leaks and even formally published reports of activities long since corrected provided enemies of America with a cornucopia of details with which to assail our country and its friends for years to come.

And selective exposure of some of intelligence's own self-criticism gave a totally false impression of American intelligence as a whole.

But intelligence did essentially succeed in protecting its individual sources and its sensitive relationships with foreign intelligence services from exposure, at the price of running battle with committees and staff members.

Did something new emerge? Yes. Intelligence has traditionally existed in a shadowy field outside the law. This ... excitement has made clear that the rule of law applies to all parts of the American government, including intelligence. In fact, this will strengthen American intelligence. Its secrets will be understood to be necessary ones for the protection of our democracy in tomorrow's world, not covers for mistake or misdeed. The guidelines within which it should, and should not, operate will be clarified for those in intelligence and those concerned about it. Improved supervision will insure that the intelligence agencies will remain within the new guidelines.

The American people will understand and support their intelligence services and press their elected representatives to give intelligence and its officers better protection from irresponsible exposure and harassment. The costs . . . were high, but they will be exceeded by the value of this strengthening of what was already the best intelligence service in the world.

CIA REFORM: HOW MUCH IS ENOUGH? [5]

The recent report of the Senate Select Committee on Intelligence Activities [the Church committee] provides an excellent basis for congressional action to reform the CIA. The President's *own* recent reorganization of the agency, however, ignores key issues that must be dealt with by Congress.

The very word *intelligence* is prejudicial in its own favor. Everyone agrees that a government should base its activities on the best available intelligence. The Central Intelligence Agency, which, as its name implies, has been the focal point for such activities within our government, has been brought into serious question. Yet it has important responsibilities which are vital to national security and must be continued. How do we separate the good in the CIA from the bad? How can we clarify, in the public mind, the difference? How can we build a new intelligence structure which can perform the essential functions with public confidence? In my view, the President's Executive order has not answered these questions.

The present agency was spawned by the Second World War. [See "Why the CIA Was Created," in Section I, above.] It was created at war's end as a "grab bag" not just for the intelligence activities of the Office of Strategic Services but for a varied group of other covert activities. Protected by wartime security, these operations had not been under normal moral, legal, or resource limitations. In retro-

[5] Guest editorial by George C. McGhee, author and former Foreign Service officer in the Department of State. *Saturday Review.* 3:5+. My. 29, '76. © 1976 by Saturday Review Associates. Reprinted by permission.

spect, it was, I believe, a mistake to have included such diverse operations under one umbrella. It was particularly misleading to call it an intelligence agency. Obviously, much of what it did went far beyond any ordinary definition of that term. Moreover, it provided continuity for wartime methods and objectives. War was succeeded by "cold war," with little change in outlook.

It should be understood, of course, that the CIA does not have a monopoly on intelligence. The Pentagon has its Defense Intelligence Agency. The Department of State, comprising some 7,500 people in Washington and 16,000 abroad, is in itself an enormous intelligence-gathering organization, not limited to its Bureau of Intelligence and Research. There is no obvious cutoff point between what should and what should not be done by the CIA. The agency has engaged in many activities, such as support for the National Student Association, because it could get the funds from Congress and State couldn't.

Nevertheless, as we continue to develop our overall intelligence capability, I believe we should also perpetuate an independent intelligence agency as a normal arm of government. There is, of course, the supporting theory that intelligence estimates by such an agency will be more objective in assessing the success or failure of policy. There is also the need for expertise and continuity in particular specialties which can perhaps best be provided by an independent agency. A case in point is the analysis of aerial photographs from satellites.

It must be emphasized, however, that most CIA intelligence gathering is, like satellite photography, quite open and aboveboard. Only the results need be kept secret. Many data are obtained from passive radio intercepts made by the military National Security Agency. Provided one has a place to put one's aerial, intercepts are an accepted tool. Often, however, in the search for intelligence, the line of legality must be breached. Covert means must be employed. Calculated risks must be taken. Spies are used. Someone is paid off. Forced entry is made. We must also protect ourselves—through counterespionage—from similar activities by other governments. In a dangerous world this is an accepted "gray" area in which all nations must compete, including, under appropriate restraints, our own intelligence agency.

Beyond this, however, as everyone knows, the CIA has been engaged in a wide range of covert activities which do not constitute intelligence collection at all; indeed, they are separated by a deep chasm. What I speak of, of course, is the whole array of covert *operational* activities, or "dirty tricks." This includes all secret attempts to manipulate the rest of the world in our favor. This is what was on trial before the Church committee and world opinion. It is these activities which have, by association, blemished CIA's legitimate intelligence function. The principal rationale, moreover, for putting them under the same roof, i.e., that the same agents do both, is not believed to be overriding. Results could be more objectively analyzed by an intelligence successor to the CIA if the two arms were separated, yet closely coordinated.

I was amazed when I came back into the State Department in 1961, after an absence of seven years, to learn the extent to which the CIA had become involved in covert activities all around the world. The Bay of Pigs operation, which lay ripe for plucking on the drawing board, was only one of many. I considered most too risky for the possible meager gains involved. We were operating in many countries. Some were close allies whose friendship we were risking. We were still supporting democratic parties in Western Europe long after the countries involved had recovered economically. Most of our operations were relatively unimportant to our national security.

When a government agency goes operational covertly,

there is, of course, a variety of choices. You start by subsidizing foreign magazines and newspapers to influence popular opinion, then progress to support for political parties and discreet bribes to officials. In the past, little attention has been paid to such activities; however, this is only the start. With know-how and funds available, you attempt to control elections, bring about the fall of governments, or even assassinate political leaders. On the macroscale this leads to what is, in effect, undeclared war. It was an open secret that in Laos the CIA for years ran a war involving large-scale air-and-ground forces. The CIA was deeply involved in Vietnam before our military took over.

When do such activities start and end? What is their proper role? How can they be controlled? I believe that responsibility for covert operational activities must be separated from the intelligence function. These operations must also be reduced greatly in scope. They must constitute the exceptional rather than the usual instrument of policy. Any decision to employ them must take into account the long-range impact on US and world opinion. People all around the world are now convinced that the CIA is manipulating their governments and people. Americans abroad are suspect as being under "cover" for CIA—our embassies, our companies, our professors, and our tourists. We are paying a high price for marginal gains.

Authority for covert operations must stem from our highest authority—the President—even if he may not always be forced to admit it. Those directing the operations must also be responsible to the Congress, preferably through one joint committee of the two houses. Every effort must be made to maintain secrecy. Guidelines must be set. Most Americans would insist, as a minimum, on a total taboo on assassination—and on undeclared war, that is, one not first approved by Congress. The joint committee itself could decide what should be approved by Congress as a whole.

The agency devoted exclusively to intelligence should be an open operation, staffed by professionals. It should need little "cover." Covert operations beyond intelligence should be conducted by some new, anonymous agency reporting directly to the President. Any undeclared wars tacitly approved by Congress should be run by a branch of the military, upon whose expertise it would draw.

Most important, however, we must understand that today's world cannot be manipulated by us in such an obvious way. A prominent CIA official once bragged to me that their operations had saved thirteen countries from communism. He did not mention countries where we are considered the enemy as a result of abortive CIA operations. We win dubiously in Chile, but we lose in Cambodia. We give Soviet arms to the Kurds and use the resulting appearance of Soviet intervention to justify furnishing arms to Iran. We give arms to Holden Roberto [anti-Communist leader] in Angola, and when the Soviet-backed Popular Front appears stronger, we feel compelled to raise the ante. What is cause and what is effect? How do you win such a game?

I recently heard a leading English journalist berate America for sabotaging our CIA just when it could have won the struggle against communism in Portugal. Does anyone really think a few million dollars can control the destiny of 10 million people?

If we are to produce the open and wise policies that will earn for us the place in the world we deserve, we must first rid ourselves of the delusion that we can win by the cheap and easy way of covert manipulation. At the same time, we must regroup and reform our varied intelligence activities—building what is appropriate into an independent and a respected arm of our government. When we venture into the murky area beyond, we should do so under new auspices, strict guidelines, and complete responsibility—not just to the President but, through the Congress, to the American

people. For it is they who will have to pay the price of any
failures, as they have done in Vietnam.

LEGISLATIVE AND EXECUTIVE ACTION NEEDED[6]

In the tempest—abundantly reported by television and
the press—that has been whirling over the heads of the intelligence community and particularly the CIA . . . ,
the accusation is frequently sounded that our intelligence
community is an unsupervised, free-wheeling body—a law
unto itself. This simply is not true. The President, himself, exercises control in a number of ways: through personal contact with his director; through the Office of Budget
and Management and a subcommittee of the National Security Council that oversees covert activities; and also
through a civilian advisory board that meets frequently, reviews the community's operations and reports to the President. The House of Representatives and the Senate have
special committees to oversee the community's activities and
to review its budgets.

For all of this extensive oversight, recent accusations of
wrongdoing—some imagined, others grossly overstated, but
still a few justified—have set up a clamor for closer supervision of the intelligence operations and especially the clandestine activities.

In my opinion, the noise has been so great and the image
of CIA has become so tarnished that changes must be made
to extinguish, as much as possible, criticism, to restore confidence and to provide an on-going dynamic foreign intelligence service. But no changes will be useful unless the
Congress, the press and electronic media, and the public can
feel assured that the nation's entire intelligence service, in
playing its part to ensure the well-being of our nation, will

[6] Excerpt from "Why We Need the CIA," by John A. McCone, CIA director
1961-1965. *TV Guide.* v 24, no 2:9-10. Ja. 10, '76. Reprinted by permission of the
author. © 1976 Triangle Publications, Inc.

always confine its operations to acceptable moral and legal standards.

The remedies involve both legislative and executive action. As we seek change, we must take great care not to damage the effectiveness of the intelligence organization and we must accept the practical truth that a foreign intelligence operation, to be effective at all, must by its very nature remain "in privacy"—its activities must be cloaked in secrecy. In a free society, we find it difficult to accept this concept, but society must accept the "cloak."

The proximity of the Central Intelligence Agency and its director to the President and the National Security Council should be made more conspicuous. Indeed, it might be advisable to identify the organization as an arm of the National Security Council and identify it that way by name. Its director would then be the nation's principal intelligence officer, with statutory authority over all of the activities now conducted by the CIA and with general supervision over the community as a whole. A subcommittee of NSC with high-level representation from State, Defense, Treasury and the White House itself, could provide a watchful eye over all intelligence activities, not merely certain covert operations as now is the case. The President's Civilian Advisory Board should continue to provide him with an informed viewpoint outside of the channels of government.

To strengthen congressional oversight, I suggest we create a single joint committee on intelligence, with membership drawn from both houses and adequately staffed. Such a committee should function in the same manner as the Joint Committee on Atomic Energy has functioned for almost thirty years. The confidentiality of all that is provided to this committee that I propose must remain within the committee, as has been the case through the years with our nuclear affairs. In particular, oversight by such a joint committee must be accepted as oversight by the Congress as a whole.

In one way or another, risks of leaks and disclosures of sensitive operations must be lessened or eliminated under severe penalties, authorized by law.

Beyond this, anyone who has been seriously connected with the responsibilities of national security will hope that our prolonged and painful review of the roles and missions of the CIA, and the work of the intelligence community as a whole, will end up by preserving an organization that can serve our security needs and yet rest comfortably within American political philosophy. Our nation would hardly be safe without such an establishment.

AMERICA'S SECRET OPERATIONS:
A PERSPECTIVE[7]

In assessing the present and future state of the AIS [American Intelligence Service], its action responsibilities provide the crucial matter for debate and decision. [AIS is sometimes known as Special Operations, Policy Coordination, Plans, Clandestine Services, or Operations. It is to be distinguished from the CIA of which it is a lesser part.] Covert action operations have declined steadily since the early 1960s outside of Indochina. Under Presidents Kennedy and Johnson, the use of covert methods to support particular candidates for office, or aspirants for power, in nations abroad became the rare exception, and today the practice has virtually died out—so that the ratio of charge to reality, in this area at least, is now extremely high. Yet the CIA charter remains in force and AIS action capabilities still exist. It is covert action—psychological, paramilitary and political—that raises not only pragmatic but political and moral issues.

Psychological warfare operations not only do not belong

[7] Excerpt from article by Harry Rositzke, former CIA officer and specialist on foreign intelligence. *Foreign Affairs.* 53:344-51. Ja. '75. Reprinted by permission from *Foreign Affairs*, January 1975. © 1974 by Council on Foreign Relations, Inc.

in a secret service, but they are an anachronism in today's world. They should be discontinued.

Paramilitary operations pose a more serious question. That the United States must keep a paramilitary capability in being for wartime use will probably not be questioned by most observers. What has become clear, however, is that a secret intelligence service is not the most suitable vehicle for running paramilitary operations. With the special privileges granted it by Congress, the CIA has been able to develop a highly efficient logistics machinery for moving personnel, equipment and funds rapidly and secretly around the world. It has therefore been called upon to carry out even large-scale paramilitary programs that would more logically fall to the Department of Defense.

There is little reason why the paramilitary charter should not be transferred to Defense, where all three services have appropriate specialized personnel, equipment and training facilities in being. All that is needed to make Defense effective in covert operations is to convert a small section of its command structure into a special operating unit which can be given congressional authority to move funds, personnel and equipment outside the bureaucratic system. This reassignment of responsibility would also bring future paramilitary operations under established congressional oversight and review.

If the AIS were to be stripped of its psychological and paramilitary operations, it could again become a truly secret service even if it retained a modified responsibility for political action.

Here, in the sphere of secret political action, the moral-political question appears to outweigh the pragmatic. How far should one nation interfere in the internal affairs of another nation?

In practice every major nation interferes daily in the affairs of other nations: by military and economic aid (or its denial), diplomatic arguments, short-wave broadcasts, fellowships and travel grants, etc. In short, Washington, like Moscow, is in this broad sense interfering all over the world all the time.

The more realistic way to phrase the issue is perhaps: to interfere *secretly*. And here no clear line can be drawn, for much of our official interference is secret: for example, the ambassador's or military attaché's private conversation with a local politician, labor leader, or general. Perhaps the issue should be even more narrowly phrased: to interfere with *money*. Yet money is involved in many acceptable forms of international dealings—travel grants, say, or American fellowships. Perhaps the issue finally becomes: to interfere with *secret money*. Put in its most loaded form: should Washington bribe a foreign politician or labor leader to act in the American interest?

Here the line between "right" and "wrong" becomes cloudy indeed. When do private understandings with a chief of state become sinister? When does the passage of money or air tickets become bribery? It is at this level that the moral issue has to be settled if it ever will be—for noninterference is one of the vaguer terms in the vocabulary of coexistence.

Should All Covert Operations Be Abandoned

It ... [has been] proposed ... that the government "should abandon publicly all covert operations designed to influence political results in foreign countries" and restore the American [intelligence] service to its original intelligence mission. (Nicholas deB. Katzenbach. "Foreign Policy, Public Opinion and Secrecy." *Foreign Affairs*, October 1973.) I would assent to this proposition with one exception and with one caveat.

The caveat first. If the President announces publicly that the CIA will no longer carry out secret political operations, no one will believe him—not the Russians, not our friends and foes around the globe, not the American public or press. "CIA" has become as much a symbol of American imperialism abroad and of secret government at home as the KGB has become, with American assistance, the symbol of Soviet imperialism and domestic repression. It is far too useful a symbol for anyone to give up, and no one will. A public statement that the US government has now returned to the path of pristine democratic practices would be a quixotic, if not a slightly humiliating, gesture.

The exception is more controversial. Propaganda and paramilitary operations do not belong in a secret service—even if they are worth doing—nor, under today's conditions, do secret operations designed to sway elections or to overturn governments. Yet the kind of clandestine intelligence contacts that are still required, simply to keep on top of complex and important situations, cannot on occasion avoid having political overtones. The justification is, as it has been, to combat what remains the very large political activity of the Soviets and their allies. Their large-scale support for political elements in many countries of the world often leaves opposing non-Communist political figures naked and without adequate support. For the United States to stay in close touch with such elements is an elemenary precaution, and there will continue to be occasions when support of a few individuals for intelligence purposes cannot (and should not) be separated from a measure of support for their political ends. There is little reason to rob the President—or the local ambassador—of the chance to provide confidential support to a politician or labor leader who cannot afford to accept American largesse publicly.

Nor can we avoid the occasional political implications of intelligence liaison relationship with the secret services of other countries, the great bulk of which are with friendly nations whose services are under proper democratic control.

In some cases such liaison has been conducted with governments whose independence has seemed, as a matter of national policy, to outweigh their failure to live up to democratic norms. It is inevitable that on occasion such governments will turn, by our standards, very sour indeed, as in the case of the Greek colonels [1967-1974], and it is a regrettable fact that an intelligence liaison aimed at external targets can then place the United States in the position of being attacked for an unintended degree of support for the local government. They key point here, however, is that intelligence liaison, like military or economic aid, is part of overall national policy, and reflects that policy: it does not normally operate in a vacuum. Indeed, in a few cases this service-to-service relationship has become the sole channel of communication with Washington for a government that has cut off diplomatic relations.

Fundamental Questions

Two fundamental questions face the AIS today: can it remain a professional service and can it become a truly secret service? Neither question can be isolated from a consideration of its structure and its mission.

Relatively modest and independent in its beginnings (as the Office of Special Operations), the AIS doubled, then tripled in size with the creation of a parallel action office (Policy Coordination) and in the overall post-Korean expansion. It went the way of the entire intelligence community: a large bureaucracy with large staffs, interminable coordination, and countless echelons of decision making.

The lethargy and timidity normal to a civil service bureaucracy exact a particularly heavy cost in an intelligence service where taking chances based on personal judgment is its main business. A service is as good as its agents, and its agents are as good as the competence and initiative of the case-officer on the spot. Faced with a hypercautious, if not anxious, headquarters, the case-officer soon learns not to take chances. He plays it safe by keeping the bread-and-butter agents he has and not invading dangerous new ground—like the local foreign office or security service. The service suffers.

As the AIS grew in size, it also became more and more closely integrated into the large-scale civil service bureaucracy that is the Central Intelligence Agency. Relatively independent at its inception, with its own administrative support structure, the AIS gradually became dependent on the CIA for its logistics, staff recruitment and training, personnel and accounting procedures, etc. Its integration into the agency was capped by the move of all CIA components into a single headquarters building in Langley, Virginia, a move strongly opposed by many senior AIS personnel on security grounds. This objection was overruled with the assurance that the larger overt agency elements would provide useful cover for the secret operators. Too many people inevitably came to know more than they needed to know about agent sources as compartmentalization broke down in the togetherness of researchers, administrators, and operators.

These, and other, considerations have led some AIS officers over the years to raise the notion of a separate truly secret intelligence service. The aim is a small elite professional service devoted exclusively to recruiting high-level agents against carefully selected long-term strategic targets. There would be no pressures for current production, no wholesale reporting requirements, no leaks to analysts, journalists or Soviet officials, no bureaucracy to hold up recruitment, no vast intelligence community to "service." Its foreign operatives would live under private, mainly commercial cover, reporting by unofficial communications to a small head office in, say, New York, whose anonymous chief would be directly responsible to the director of Central Intelligence in his capacity as the President's head of the intelligence community.

The present Operations Directorate of the CIA would remain the integral part of the intelligence community it has become. It cannot be extracted from its present structure—as, for example, it would be administratively simple to extract the Federal Bureau of Investigation from the Department of Justice. Nor should it be. Although the Operations Directorate would no longer be depended upon to provide agent coverage of strategic intelligence targets, it would continue to function abroad on a reduced scale and with a more innocuous mission: to maintain liaison with local security and intelligence services, to protect the Embassy from hostile penetration, to handle agent or defector walk-ins. It would also serve as a channel for confidential communications between the ambassador and the President or between the host government and the State Department, and supply local support for other elements of the intelligence community, including the National Security Agency, the military services, and the FBI. Wherever feasible, and with deference to the sensitivities of the local situation, the CIA station chief might be overtly accredited as the CIA representative. He would, in any event, act as the ambassador's overall assistant for intelligence matters.

However quixotic on the surface, a small American secret service separate from the federal bureaucracy is not at all impractical—given the will in high places. The concept of such a service is not too far removed from the Soviet system of illegals: carefully selected personnel, hand-tailored communications, small-scale operations, select priority targets. It would remain professional and secret.

The present Central Intelligence Agency, shorn of its strategic espionage mission, would not be affected in its structure or main functions. It would continue to carry out its overt and technical collection operations, to provide its extensive services of common concern to the entire intelligence community, and to do current and in-depth analysis and research. It would, above all, continue to focus on its main *central* function—to give the White House intelligence estimates on situations and trends abroad that are as objective as men can make them. Only an agency exclusively concerned with intelligence can avoid the intrusion of bias into honest judgments that comes from the pressure in the Departments of State or Defense to support a specific diplomatic tack or a larger military budget.

This proposal would simplify the vexing issue of congressional oversight. With overt and unexceptionable covert activities more clearly separated from truly covert ones, the supervision of the CIA itself would be substantially freed of the fear of exposing those operations that almost all members of Congress agree should remain secret. Present committees could thus operate more effectively. The truly secret operations of the AIS might best be reviewed by an ad hoc group of the top majority and minority members of the key committees who would weigh the policy implications, not the operating details, of the secret program.

Setting up a separate espionage service is only one side, and the simpler side, of the problem. What would be its mission? What targets would it be directed to cover that would justify its cost?

Sensibly limiting information requirements could halve the size of the intelligence community devoted to collection. Only against a clear-cut yardstick of essential information can a congressional oversight group or a presidential advisory group measure the effectiveness of our intelligence effort. With covert psychological warfare a relic of the past, with paramilitary operations (if any) handled by the Pentagon and subject to the usual congressional scrutiny, with secret political actions carried out only at the express direction of the National Security Council, there would remain only the espionage and counterespionage operations of the new AIS for the Congress to "oversee." And here the task should be to test performance by the product: raw agent reports measured against the government's requirements.

Requirements properly come from outside the intelligence community. Intelligence exists to serve the decision makers, and agent reports (ideally) fill the gaps in other coverage. For a small strategic AIS to carry out operations of real value requires that the policymakers project with some concreteness their foreign policy objectives well into the eighties. Only then can they articulate, by countries or categories of information, their priority intelligence targets. As the simple confrontations of the cold war give way to the more complex alignments of today, as economic and fiscal questions replace military hardware as topics of major interest, the intelligence needs of the White House are bound to shift. Is the Tokyo-Moscow axis a top priority? Are the Swiss bankers—or the German industrialists—a more important target than the Chinese General Staff?

Who Is to Answer?

Who will answer these questions?

It is possible, in a sanguine moment, to see a select joint congressional committee sitting down with the National Security Council and talking about the problems America faces in the decades ahead. They should confer until they come up with a clear statement in simple English of our long-term national objectives and a concrete list of specific areas and countries vital to our nation's interest.

In an even more sanguine moment one can envisage a broader, more representative body sitting down every two or three years and examining the *performance* of our foreign affairs and intelligence activities abroad. Such a group, chaired by the Vice President and supported by the National Security Council's administrative machinery, would ideally include not only congressmen, but security-cleared citizens from business, labor, the media, academia. Their report to the American people might add a welcome breath of fresh air to the stale words from Washington.

Any decisions on our purposes in this faltering world can come only from the top and not out of the bowels of our foreign affairs bureaucracies. And those decisions cannot come by two-year or four-year Executive fiat. They should be reached with the widest possible participation. . . . [Gerald Ford] with his close ties to Congress is the ideal man to broaden the base for Executive decisions in foreign policy. He should take the initiative in inviting the Congress to share his "awesome" responsibility for foreign affairs—perhaps even go so far as to first invite a systematic national debate. He can raise the level of that debate by being more open with the public on now-classified intelligence available within the Executive branch. There is much to be gained, and—properly screened—little to be lost by publishing some of our excellent satellite photographs, or select national estimates on strategic situations as they arise, or current intelligence reports on significant events abroad.

The system of American democracy need not be exhausted by its present institutions, nor should the citizen sit on his hands as the complex pressures of an industrial society force the cancerous growth of the Executive. No President in the future should be allowed to say on his own that the Dominican Republic or Cuba or Vietnam is vital to the American interest.

Once set, and amended, long-term national objectives lead to strategic intelligence as well as diplomatic targets, to a clean-cut mission for the new AIS. It is likely that these targets may lie in Zurich and Tokyo as well as Moscow or Bucharest or Cairo and concern themselves as much with goods and currencies as with war and politics. It is even possible that the AIS might on occasion, like the KGB in the recent Soviet grain deal, pay for its own budget by saving the taxpayer money.

BIBLIOGRAPHY

An asterisk (*) preceding a reference indicates that the article or a part of it has been reprinted in this book.

BOOKS AND DOCUMENTS

Barron, John. KGB; the secret work of Soviet secret agents. Reader's Digest Press. '73.

Blackstock, P. W. The strategy of subversion; manipulating the politics of other nations. Quadrangle. '64.

*Dulles, A. W. The craft of intelligence. Harper. '63.

Felix, Christopher, pseud. A short course in the secret war. Dutton. '63.

Gramont, Sanche de. The secret war; the story of international espionage since World War II. Putnam. '62.

Hilman, Roger. Strategic intelligence and national decisions. Free Press. '56.

*Kent, Sherman. Strategic intelligence for American world policy. Princeton University Press. '49.

Kirkpatrick, L. B. Jr. The real CIA. Macmillan. '68.

Pettee, G. S. The future of American secret intelligence. Infantry Journal Press. '46.

Ransom, H. H. Can American democracy survive the cold war? Doubleday. '63.

*Ransom, H. H. The intelligence establishment. Harvard University Press. '70.

Rowan, R. W. and Deindorfer, R.G. Secret service: 33 centuries of espionage. New & rev ed Hawthorne Books. '67.
1st edition published by Doubleday under title: The story of secret service.

United States. Commission on CIA Activities Within the United States. Report to President, June 1975. Supt. of Docs. Washington, D.C. 20402. '75.

United States. Congress. National security act of 1947: unification of the armed services. (P.L. 80-253) Cornell Law Library. Ithaca, NY 14850. '47.

United States. Congress. House. Select Committee on Intelligence. U.S. intelligence and activities: intelligence and fiscal procedures; hearings held July 31-August 8, 1975. 94th Congress; 1st Session. U.S. Gov. Ptg. Office. Washington, D.C. 20401. '75-

United States. Congress. Senate. Select Committee to Study Governmental Operations With Respect to Intelligence Activities. Alleged assassination plots involving foreign leaders; an interim report; together with additional, supplemental, and separate views; foreword by Clark R. Mollenhoff; introd. by Sen. Frank Church. Norton. '76.

*United States. Congress. Senate. Select Committee to Study Governmental Operations With Respect to Intelligence Activities. Report on foreign and military intelligence activities of the United States. (Senate Doc. No. 94-755) Supt. of Docs. Washington, D.C. 20402. '76. 6v.

Zlotnick, Jack. National intelligence. (U.S. Industrial College of the Armed Forces. The Economics of National Security) Washington, D.C. '64.

PERIODICALS

America. 131:314. N. 23, '74. Missionaries and the CIA.

America. 134:204-6. Mr. 13, '76. Doing away with covert activities. B. J. O'Connell.

Atlantic. 237:31-42. Ap. '76. Intelligence tangle: the CIA and the FBI face the moment of truth. S. J. Ungar.

Biblical Society. 12:7-8+, 26-80. Mr. '75. Espionage: U.S. [symposium with editorial comment]

Bulletin of the Atomic Scientists. 32:7-11. F. '76. Covert action: swampland of American foreign policy. Frank Church.

*Columbia Today. v 2, no 1:6-9. Je. '76. Can our freedoms survive defense by the CIA and FBI (Columbia Law Symposium).

Current. 173:3-6. My. '75. Spying and security. I. L. Horowitz.

Department of State Bulletin. 74:274-7. Mr. 1, '76. Congress and the U.S. intelligence community; statement, February 5, 1976. H. A. Kissinger.

Ebony. 31:42. Mr. '76. Probing the intelligence community. R. V. Dellums.

*Foreign Affairs. 53:334-51. Ja. '75. America's secret operations: a perspective. H. A. Rositzke.

Foreign Affairs. 54:482-95. Ap. '76. Is espionage necessary for our security? Herbert Scoville Jr.

*Freedom at Issue. no 35:3-7. Mr.-Ap. '76. Intelligence, morality and foreign policy. Sidney Hook.

Intellect. 104:426-8. Mr. '76. Reforming the CIA. R. C. Gray.

Nation. 220:363-9. Mr. 29, '75. Behind the CIA: emergence of the dual state. Alan Wolfe.

Nation. 220:546. My. 10, '75. X factor; CIA personnel and performance.

Nation. 221:98-9. Ag. 16, '75. Foreign Watergates; collaboration between CIA and American multinational corporations in foreign intrigues.

Nation. 221:108-12. Ag. 16, '75. Exercise in gentility: The Rockefeller CIA report. Alan Wolfe.

Nation. 222:138-40. F. 7, '76. Intelligence: the test for Congress. Michael Harrington.

Nation. 222:386-8. Ap. 3, '76. Intelligence and horse sense.

National Review. 27:302. Mr. 14, '75. Assault on the CIA. W. F. Buckley Jr.

National Review. 28:254-5. Mr. 19, '76. Who is to watch the watchmen?

New Republic. 172:7-8. Ja. 4, '75. Checking the CIA.

New Republic. 172:10-12. F. 1, '75. Covering intelligence; New York Times coverage of Central Intelligence Agency operations. Walter Pincus.

New York Times. p 43. My. 17, '73. Sen. Symington charges White House aides with enlisting CIA help.

New York Times. p 51. My. 20, '73. M. H. Halperin charges CIA as "self serving and unreserved danger" to U.S.

New York Times. p 5. Ag. 21, '73. CIA undergoes major organizational change—first in ten years.

New York Times. sec IV, p 2. N. 4, '73. House Armed Services Subcommittee cite CIA for allowing itself to be used for "improper purposes."

New York Times. p 8. Je. 7, '74. Major changes in CIA begun by new director Colby.

New York Times. p 4. Jl. 12, '74. Ex-CIA staff officer Philip Agee explains why he decided to make public CIA operations.

New York Times. p 1. S. 17, '74. President Ford outlines support of CIA clandestine ops for national security.

New York Times. p 11. S. 20, '74. Senators Weicker and Baker present bill to create joint congressional oversight committee.

New York Times. p 1. D. 22, '74. Government sources report CIA conducted massive illegal domestic intelligence operation. S. M. Hersh.

New York Times. p 16. Ja. 1, '75. Colby confirms maintenance of files on U.S. citizens and program of surveillance break-ins etc. inside U.S.

New York Times. p 1. Ja. 5, '75. President Ford establishes committee to investigate allegations of domestic spying by CIA—Rockefeller heads.

New York Times. p 1. Ja. 10, '75. CIA counterintelligence division alleged to have sought destruction of own files on Americans to prevent disclosure.

New York Times. sec IV, p 1. Ja. 12, '75. Review of congressional inability to oversee and other basic problems controlling CIA.

New York Times. sec IV, p 4. Ja. 12, '75. Reviews origins CIA and statutory limitations and CIA actions contrary authorization. David Wise.

New York Times. p 1. Ja. 16, '75. Colby acknowledges CIA infiltration domestic political groups, Senator Proxmire calls for establishment Senate select committee.

New York Times. p 1. F. 20, '75. House votes to establish Select Committee on Intelligence.

New York Times. p 1. Mr. 5, '75. Colby reports to President Ford on past assassination plans of CIA.

New York Times. p 1. Mr. 15, '75. Senate Select Committee asks White House for information on foreign and domestic intelligence activities of the past five presidents.

New York Times. p 20. Mr. 16, '75. International security experts defend CIA covert activities at CCNY conference.

New York Times. sec IV, p 19. Mr. 16, '75. Hope for effective CIA is clean-sweep current leadership and creation powerful congressional oversight. James Reston.

New York Times. p 26. Ap. 12, '75. Editorial notes special status of intelligence agency demands punctilious obeying spirit as well as letter of their mandate.

New York Times. p 9. Ap. 16, '75. White House turns over Colby secret CIA report on its operations to Senate Intelligence Committee.

New York Times. p 8. My. 16, '75. Colby gives Senate Intelligence Committee overview of CIA covert operations for last thirty years.

New York Times. p 42. My. 18, '75. Senator Church outlines philosophy behind Senate Intelligence Committee investigations.

New York Times. p 18. Je. 11, '75. Text of summary, Rockefeller CIA Committee Report.

New York Times. p 1. Je. 19, '75. Authoritative source states CIA organized Castro assassination attempt and names Mafia figures and CIA officers involved.

New York Times. p 1. Jl. 9, '75. CIA makes public report of its domestic intelligence build-up in Nixon years, started during Johnson Administration.

New York Times. p 6. Jl. 18, '75. House abolishes its Intelligence Committee chaired by Rep. Nedzi, replaces it with new expanded committee chaired by Rep. Otis Pike.

New York Times. p 1. Ag. 3, '75. FBI charged with operations begun in early '50's of compiling secret list of American citizens as possible wartime security risks.

New York Times. p 1. Ag. 31, '75. National Security Agency (NSA) charged with eavesdropping on virtually all international communications to/fro the U.S.

New York Times. p 1. S. 25, '75. Senate Intelligence Committee discloses CIA has been opening foreign correspondence to/fro top citizens for twenty years.

New York Times. p 21. O. 10, '75. Analysis of ongoing congressional intelligence probes indicates investigators overwhelmed with task and data—now unsure of objective. N. M. Horrock.

New York Times. p 1. N. 4, '75. President Ford names George Bush to replace CIA director William Colby.

New York Times. p 1. N. 10, '75. Survey of impact of Congressional investigations on CIA current operations.

New York Times. p 50. N. 21, '75. Text of Senate Intelligence Committee reports U.S. Gov't officials investigating assassination operations.

*New York Times. sec IV, p 17. N. 23, '75. The dark at the top. Tom Wicker.

New York Times. p 1. D. 4, '75. Senate Intelligence Committee charges FBI used by all Presidents from F. D. Roosevelt to Nixon to supply political information on rivals.

New York Times. p 33. Ja. 13, '76. Reasons for prohibiting covert operations. Tom Wicker.

New York Times. p 1. Ja. 15, '76. Senator Church discusses future role of possible new joint congressional oversight committee on intelligence.

New York Times. p 1. Ja. 21, '76. Justice Department states no grounds exist for prosecution CIA officials involved in assassination foreign leader plots.

New York Times. p 1. Ja. 30, '76. House votes to withhold publication final report Pike Intelligence Committee until Executive branch reviews.

*New York Times. sec IV, p 1. F. 1, '76. A few in Congress could see what the spooks were doing. N. M. Horrock.

New York Times. p 24. F. 8, '76. House Intelligence Committee passes recommendations for future controls.

*New York Times. p 13. F. 15, '76. World nation-state structure makes intelligence essential. Lord Chalfont (Alun Gwynne-Jones).
Reprinted from the Times of London.

New York Times. p 1. F. 18, '76. President Ford announces "sweeping" general reformation of national intelligence structure.

New York Times. p 1. F. 19, '76. Presidential order details restriction of intelligence agency power.

*New York Times. p 25. F. 23, '76. Laws, men and the CIA. Anthony Lewis.

*New York Times. p 31. F. 26, '76. After investigating U.S. intelligence. W. E. Colby.

New York Times. p 1. Ap. 27, '76. Senate Select Committee on Intelligence issues final report after fifteen months of study.

New York Times. p 1. My. 12, '76. Senate leaders agree on plan to create permanent new Senate Intelligence Committee.

*New York Times. p 20. My. 12, '76. Spy inquiries, begun in outrage, end in indifference. L. H. Gelb.

New York Times. p 1. My. 20, '76. Senate votes establishment permanent Select Committee on Intelligence with exclusive oversight authority.

New York Times. p 27. My. 21, '76. Senate action on intelligence shows ability of Congress to take proper actions when needed. James Reston.

New York Times Magazine. p 10-11+. D. 21, '75. Should we play dirty tricks in the world? L. H. Gelb.

New York Times Magazine. p 35+. S. 12, '76. The trial of the C.I.A. Taylor Branch.

New Yorker. 51:165-70. N. 3, '75. Letter from Washington. R. H. Rovere.

Newsweek. 85:11. Ap. 7, '75. Abolish the CIA! A. J. Langguth.

Newsweek. 85:13. Ap. 28, '75. God bless the CIA. Peer De Silva.

Newsweek. 85:16-18. Je. 23, '75. Cloak comes off. Peter Goldman and others.

Newsweek. 85:19-22+. Je. 23, '75. Who's watching whom? D. M. Alpern and others.

Newsweek. 86:27-8. D. 15, '75. It all began with FDR; FBI's political intelligence gathering. Sandra Salmans and Stephan Lesher.

Newsweek. 87:18-19. Mr. 1, '76. Ford's CIA shake-up. D. M. Alpern and others.

Newsweek. 87:40+. My. 10, '76. Inquest on Intelligence; final report. D. M. Alpern and others.

Progressive. 39:35-9. F. '75. Partners: labor and the CIA. Sidney Lens.

Progressive. 40:5-6. Mr. '76. We must know everything. J. A. McCone.

Progressive. 40:8-9. My. '76. Congress and the CIA. L. J. Paper.

Reader's Digest. 108:101-5. My. '76. Let's stop undermining the CIA. M. R. Laird.

Saturday Review. 2:14-18. Ap. 5, '75. What's wrong with the CIA? Tom Braden.

Saturday Review. 2:4. Ag. 9, '75. American traditions and secret police. Norman Cousins.

*Saturday Review. 3:5+. My. 29, '76. CIA reform: how much is enough? G. C. McGhee.

*TV Guide. v 24, no 2:6-10. Ja. 10, '76. Why we need the CIA. J. A. McCone.

Time. 105:31-2. Ja. 20, '75. Examining the examiners.

Time. 105:32. Ja. 20, '75. Another look at the CIA. Hugh Sidney.

Time. 105:6-10+. Je. 23, '75. Rocky's probe; bringing the CIA to heel.

Time. 106:24+. S. 29, '75. Toward restoring the necessary CIA [essay]. Strobe Talbott.

Time. 106:14. N. 10, '75. NSA: inside the puzzle palace.

Time. 107:20. My. 31, '76. Watchdog at last; Senate vote to establish a permanent committee to oversee all intelligence bureaus.

U.S. News & World Report. 77:29-32+. D. 2, '74. Spotlight on the CIA; interview. W. E. Colby.

U.S. News & World Report. 78:51-2. Ja. 6, '75. CIA scandal—and the backlash.

U.S. News & World Report. 78:18. Ja. 13, '75. How troubles will change the CIA.

U.S. News & World Report. 78:22-3. Ja. 20, '75. Probing the CIA —investigators under fire.

U.S. News & World Report. 78:33. Je. 16, '75. CIA and assassination plots—Rockefeller report stirs furor.

U.S. News & World Report. 79:39. Ag. 25, '75. CIA: best in world.

U.S. News & World Report. 80:20. Ja. 12, '76. Secrecy, dirty tricks at heart of CIA battle.

U.S. News & World Report. 80:23-4. My. 10, '76. Reform of the CIA—what it really boils down to. Joseph Fromm.

Wall Street Journal. p 8. Jl. 2, '75. "What about the CIA?" Arthur Schlesinger.

*Wall Street Journal. p 18. F. 24, '76. Wrong problem at CIA [editorial].